FORTRESS • 97

COLDITZ: OFLAG IV-C

MICHAEL McNALLY

ILLUSTRATED BY PETER DENNIS

Series editor Marcus Cowper

First published in 2010 by Osprey Publishing
Midland House, West Way, Botley, Oxford OX2 0PH, UK
44-02 23rd St, Suite 219, Long Island City, NY 11101, USA
E-mail: info@ospreypublishing.com

ISBN: 978 1 84603 583 8
E-book ISBN: 978 1 84908 291 4

Editorial by Ilios Publishing Ltd, Oxford, UK (www.iliospublishing.com)
Cartography: Map Studio, Romsey, UK
Page layout by Ken Vail Graphic Design, Cambridge, UK (kvgd.com)
Typeset in Myriad and Sabon
Index by Alison Worthington
Originated by PDQ Digital Media Solutions Ltd, Suffolk, Uk

Printed in China through Bookbuilders

10 11 12 13 14   10 9 8 7 6 5 4 3 2 1

A CIP catalogue record for this book is available from the British Library.

FOR A CATALOGUE OF ALL BOOKS PUBLISHED BY OSPREY MILITARY
AND AVIATION PLEASE CONTACT:

Osprey Direct, c/o Random House Distribution Center,
400 Hahn Road, Westminster, MD 21157
Email: uscustomerservice@ospreypublishing.com

Osprey Direct, The Book Service Ltd, Distribution Centre,
Colchester Road, Frating Green, Colchester, Essex, CO7 7DW
E-mail: customerservice@ospreypublishing.com

www.ospreypublishing.com

DEDICATION

As always, I'd like to firstly thank my wife – Petra – and children – Stephen,
Elena and Liam – for their forbearance and understanding throughout this
whole project. I'd also like to take this opportunity to thank a number of
people whose own contributions have been crucial. Firstly, my editors:
Marcus Cowper, both for his continual support and for his agreement to my
original proposal, and Christopher Pannell for taking over the project 'mid
term'; and also Andy Copestake, Martin Francis, Lee Offen, Thomas Brogan,
Seán Ó'Brógáin and Ian Spence for their constructive proofreading of the
manuscript. Special thanks also to Peter Dennis for breathing life into my
suggestions and creating some truly evocative artwork.

My special thanks also to Dr François Wisard, head of the History Unit of the
Federal Department of Foreign Affairs in Berne, for his kind assistance in
answering my queries regarding both the 3rd Geneva Convention and the
role of Switzerland as a 'Protecting Power' during World War II.

In the town of Colditz itself I'd like to express my gratitude to both Regina
Thiede and Steffi Schubert of the Gesellschaft Schloss Colditz e.V. for their
exceptional help and assistance during my visit to the castle and to Ralf
Gorny, proprietor of the Pension "Alte Stadtmauer" for his kind hospitality
and advice.

Finally I'd like to thank the staffs of the Imperial War Museum in London,
and the Australian War Memorial in Canberra for their kind assistance in
sourcing and granting permission for a number of contemporary images
reproduced within this book.

ARTIST'S NOTE

Readers may care to note that the original paintings from which the
colour plates in this book were prepared are available for private sale.
All reproduction copyright whatsoever is retained by the Publishers. All
enquiries should be addressed to:

Peter Dennis, Fieldhead, The Park, Mansfield, NG18 2AT

The Publishers regret that they can enter into no correspondence upon
this matter.

IMPERIAL WAR MUSEUM COLLECTIONS

Many of the photos in this book come from the Imperial War Museum's
huge collections, which cover all aspects of conflict involving Britain and
the Commonwealth since the start of the twentieth century. These rich
resources are available online to search, browse and buy at
www.iwmcollections.org.uk. In addition to collections online, you can
visit the visitor rooms where you can explore over 8 million photographs,
thousands of hours of moving images, the largest sound archive of its kind
in the world, thousands of diaries and letters written by people in wartime,
and a huge reference library. To make an appointment, call (020) 7416
5320, or e-mail mail@iwm.org.uk. Imperial War Museum www.iwm.org.uk

THE FORTRESS STUDY GROUP (FSG)

The object of the FSG is to advance the education of the public in the
study of all aspects of fortifications and their armaments, especially
works constructed to mount or resist artillery. The FSG holds an annual
conference in September over a long weekend with visits and evening
lectures, an annual tour abroad lasting about eight days, and an annual
Members' Day.

The FSG journal FORT is published annually, and its newsletter Casemate
is published three times a year. Membership is international. For further
details, please contact:

secretary@fsgfort.com

Website: www.fsgfort.com

THE HISTORY OF FORTIFICATION STUDY CENTRE (HFSC)

The History of Fortification Study Centre (HFSC) is an international scientific
research organization that aims to unite specialists in the history of military
architecture from antiquity to the 20th century (including historians, art
historians, archaeologists, architects and those with a military background).
The centre has its own scientific council, which is made up of authoritative
experts who have made an important contribution to the study of
fortification.

The HFSC's activities involve organizing conferences, launching research
expeditions to study monuments of defensive architecture, contributing
to the preservation of such monuments, arranging lectures and special
courses in the history of fortification and producing published works such
as the refereed academic journal Questions of the History of Fortification,
monographs and books on the history of fortification. It also holds a
competition for the best publication of the year devoted to the history
of fortification.

The headquarters of the HFSC is in Moscow, Russia, but the centre is
active in the international arena and both scholars and amateurs from all
countries are welcome to join. More detailed information about the HFSC
and its activities can be found on the website: www.hfsc.3dn.ru

E-mail: ciif-info@yandex.ru

THE WOODLAND TRUST

Osprey Publishing are supporting the Woodland Trust, the UK's leading
woodland conservation charity, by funding the dedication of trees.

CONTENTS

COLDITZ: OFLAG IV-C

INTRODUCTION

Although outside Germany Colditz is most commonly known for the castle's use as a prisoner of war (POW) camp during World War II, this is but a small excerpt in a varied and colourful history stretching back for over a thousand years into the early decades of the Holy Roman Empire.

According to local legend, shortly before his death Count Eckhard II von Meissen bequeathed his lands to the Holy Roman Emperor Henry III who, in turn, and aware of the pressing need to place the border province in trustworthy hands, then granted virtually the whole bequest to one of his principal advisers, Wilhelm IV of Weimar-Orlamünde. The exception to this was the Slavic settlement of Choliditscha – later Germanized as 'Colditz' – in the valley of the river Mulde, which Henry settled upon his wife, Agnès of Poitou, for her future financial security.

The north-west face of Colditz taken from the slopes of the Hainberg. The German married quarters and entrance to the park are to the left of the image, and the town itself is to the right. (Author)

Within a few short decades, this endowment had developed into an integral part of the *Ostsiedlung* – the Germanic settlement of the Slavic lands on the eastern borders of the Empire – and as the process of Teutonic colonization continued, a castle or *Burg* was built on the cliffs overlooking the settlement.

Succeeding centuries saw Colditz twice gutted by fire, but she rose from the ashes each time, ultimately being enlarged and redeveloped, so that by the 1600s the castle had been established as a royal residence, remaining in the hands of the electoral family until the mid-18th century when its contents were auctioned off to the public and the buildings handed over to the state for use by the ever-growing government bureaucracy.

Eventually the bureaucrats left Colditz for the cities of Dresden and Leipzig, and after another period of neglect it reopened as a poorhouse cum workhouse and then psychiatric hospital for the Leipzig area that remained in service until its closure in 1924. This penultimate period of hiatus ensued until 1933, when the newly elected National Socialist government used Colditz as a security camp to house opponents of the regime.

After World War II, Colditz was initially used by the Soviets as a camp for displaced persons, and after its handover to the fledgling German Democratic Republic it became once again a hospital. It fulfilled this role for almost half a century until 1996, at which time an association – the Gesellschaft Schloss Colditz e.V – was formed with the aim of restoring the castle to its former glory, a role in which, in conjunction with federal and regional government, it continues to this day.

CHRONOLOGY

1046	Emperor Henry III presents his wife with the title to Colditz.
1083	Wiprecht von Groitzsch receives the title to Colditz from Emperor Henry IV.
1158	Colditz becomes an imperial fief under Thimo I von Wettin.
1200	A town is established below the castle.
1404	The title to Colditz passes from the von Wettin family to the Marquisate of Meissen.
1430	Hussites sack Colditz, burning the town and castle, which lie in ruins for over 30 years.
1464	The Elector of Saxony rebuilds the castle as one of his principal residences.
1504	The town and castle are gutted by an accidental fire that begins in a local bakery.
1586	The castle is renovated and rebuilt as a royal hunting lodge.
1753	The castle falls into disrepair with remaining effects being sold at auction in 1787.
1800	Colditz is converted into a poorhouse for the Leipzig region.
1829	Establishment of an asylum within the castle precincts.
1924	The asylum is shut down.

1933	Colditz is used as a prison for political opponents of the Nazi regime.
1939	Colditz is established as a POW camp under the designation Oflag IV-C.
1945	Colditz is liberated by US forces.
1946	The castle reverts to use firstly as a hospital and then as a nursing home.
1996	Foundation of the Gesellschaft Schloss Colditz e.V.

DESIGN AND DEVELOPMENT

Although there are no extant descriptions of the original fortification built above the town of Colditz, it is certain that in common with known castles of the period it would have consisted of an embanked wooden palisade (*Burgwall*) surrounding a wooden tower (*Bergfried*) rising to a height at least twice that of the palisade, and in profile it would not have been unlike a Norman 'motte and bailey' castle.

As a minor outpost on the Empire's eastern borders, and located in the northern part of the clifftop plateau, the castle's wooden defences were eminently suitable for the purpose for which they were constructed – relatively cheap and easy to maintain, their presence high above the river Mulde not only gave the local inhabitants a sense of protection but also served to act as a focal point for smaller outlying settlements.

This close-up of Colditz shows perfectly how the castle dominates the town, and especially the central marketplace, which lies directly below the castle eminence. (Author)

The growth of medieval Saxony to 1485

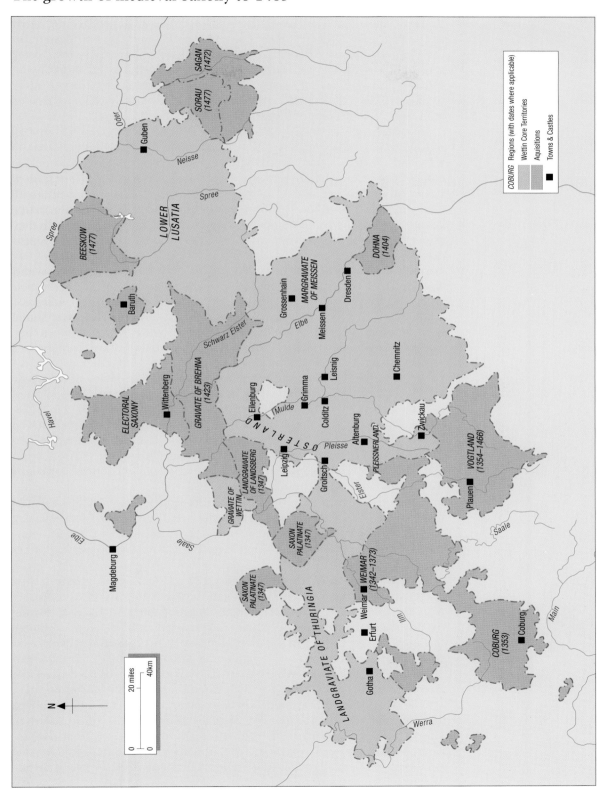

Legend:
- *COBURG* Regions (with dates where applicable)
- Wettin Core Territories
- Aquisitions
- Towns & Castles

SAGAN (1472)
SORAU (1477)
Guben
Oder
Neisse
Spree
LOWER LUSATIA
Spree
BEESKOW (1477)
Spree
Baruth
Schwarz Elster
Grossenhain
MARGRAVATE OF MEISSEN
Dresden
DOHNA (1404)
Meissen
Elbe
Chemnitz
Leisnig
Eilenburg
Grimma
ELECTORAL SAXONY
Wittenberg
GRAVIATE OF BREHNA (1423)
Mulde
Colditz
Zwickau
Havel
OSTERLAND
Altenburg
PLEISSNERLAND
VOGTLAND (1354–1466)
LANDGRAVIATE OF LANDSBERG (1347)
Leipzig
Groitsch
Pleisse
Elster
Plauen
GRAVIATE OF WETTIN
Saale
Elbe
Saale
SAXON PALATINATE (1347)
Magdeburg
SAXON PALATINATE (1347)
WEIMAR (1342–1373)
Saale
Weimar
Ilm
Erfurt
COBURG (1353)
Coburg
Main
LANDGRAVIATE OF THURINGIA
Gotha
Werra

20 miles
40km
N

As the 11th century drew to a close, a coalition of disaffected nobles led by the charismatic Rudolf von Rheinfelden rose up in rebellion against Emperor Henry IV. The subsequent rout of the imperial army at the battle of the Elster in October 1080 should have ended matters, but, despite his crushing victory, von Rheinfelden was mortally wounded during the closing stages of the battle and his death denied the rebels the fruits of their hard-won victory. This also gave the battered emperor an unlooked-for opportunity to re-establish his authority and stabilize his position by placing trusted adherents in possession of a number of strategic castles.

In 1084, one of these – Wiprecht von Groitzsch – received control of Colditz and its dependencies. Ironically, von Groitzsch was himself a Saxon who had previously been forced into exile as a result of his unscrupulous colonization of the Meissen area, and thus armed with imperial favour he now began an even more ambitious programme, repopulating his lands with Germans from Franconia. With an eye to defence and with his newly acquired possessions spread over a number of disparate fiefdoms, von Groitzsch then began the refurbishment of a number of castles, gradually replacing the timber defences with more durable stonework. Regrettably, little or no trace of von Groitzsch's castle remains at Colditz, with the exception of the ruins of a pillared rotunda that were found underneath the prospective site of the altar when the castle chapel was being built, and some half-buried walls and scattered glasswork dating to the 11th and 12th centuries that were found during the excavation of the *Kellerhaus*. It can therefore only be assumed that, in common with the practice of the time, existing stonework was cannibalized and incorporated into the later construction.

At the beginning of the 12th century, physical possession of the castle subsequently came into the hands of a Saxon knight named Boppo who, assuming the title 'von Colditz', created the line of future counts. In 1158, during the reign of the Emperor Frederick I 'Barbarossa', Colditz became an imperial fief and Boppo's grandson, Count Thimo von Wettin, henceforward Thimo I von Colditz, was elevated to the membership of the imperial court and confirmed in a possession that his successors would continue to occupy for the following 400 years.

Below the castle and in the shadow of the clifftop fortress, the town of Colditz also grew, and what had originally been a collection of ramshackle huts developed into a burgeoning town, characterized by the many new buildings built around a central market square, a positive indication of her increasing prosperity.

Although the reconstruction of Colditz as a stone castle has been a slow and extended affair, archaeologists have been able to identify two distinct periods of rebuilding. The former dates approximately to 1323, following the accession of the 13-year-old Frederick II as Count of Meissen. Although this may have been part of a general rebuilding programme, in the power politics of the time the accession of a minor invariably caused a realignment of political factions, and adherents of the new ruler would need to ensure that his inheritance could be adequately defended against any and all enemies.

The second phase of growth has been dated to 1362 and can be said to mark the final stages of the construction of the medieval castle. It was, however, a form that would remain intact for less than three generations as militant agitation for religious reform by the nobility of Bohemia and Moravia developed into a conflict that raged across the countryside for over a decade of almost constant warfare.

This view of a barred window shaft illustrates the depth of the castle walls, which in places reach a thickness of 3–4m. (Author)

Over the next two years these pinpricks became a concentrated offensive as Hussite forces marched northwards adopting a policy of bypassing centres of resistance and engaging only soft targets, and, around 1430, with the Saxon army primarily covering Leipzig, a column of Hussite troops moving northwards along the Mulde valley came upon Colditz, sacking both town and castle and leaving a trail of ruin and destruction in its wake.

The peace signed with the Hussites in 1434 following the battle of Cesky Brod proved to be a fragile one when the early death of one of the brothers and the forced entry into the Church of another left but two contenders for the electoral throne, and as a result Saxony was wracked by five years of civil war until the eldest, Frederick, emerged victorious and commenced his 20-year reign as sole elector.

Despite the years of desolation, the fortunes of Colditz were revived somewhat in 1464 with the accession of Frederick's two sons, Ernest and Albert, who ruled co-jointly for two decades until 1485 when the realm was formally divided into the Electoral Dignity, which was ruled from the city of Wittenberg, and the Duchy of Saxony, which was ruled from Dresden. As the eldest, Ernest was confirmed as the *Kurfürst* or electoral prince, whilst his brother, Albert, acceded to the ducal title. Known as the 'Partition of Leipzig', this territorial division effectively established two ruling houses in the principality – the Ernestines and the Albertines – and thus two rival factions in constant competition for the electoral title.

Having been born in nearby Meissen, Ernest showed a clear interest in the local area and his reconstruction of Burg Colditz as a royal hunting lodge effectively marks the foundation of the modern castle, being based around what are now the four principal buildings of the inner courtyard or *Innenhof*, all of which were increased in height with the construction of additional storeys.

Until now, both the electors and their attendants would be accommodated in what was to become the *Kellerhaus* or buttery, but Ernest decided that his status required something grander and the existing buildings on the opposite (eastern) side of the courtyard were demolished, and in their place was to rise

The western profile of Colditz Castle. (Author)

a new edifice, the *Fürstenhaus*, which was thereafter to serve as the private residence of the electoral family. Linking these two buildings, and initially unconnected to either of them, was the castle chapel or *Schlosskapelle*. Finally, the quadrangle was completed by the refurbishment of the Great Hall or *Saalhaus* where guests would be entertained.

It should be stressed that Ernest's reconstruction of the complex effectively marked the transition of Colditz from a military strongpoint to a formal residence, and this is reflected in the title '*Schloss*' which was conferred upon the castle to mark its new, royal status. Although still an imposing edifice, with outer walls between 3.5–4.5m thick, it is assumed that any remaining defensive works such as crenellations were now modified to better support the roofed upper stories that were added at this time along with the *Altan* or *Söller*, an exterior platform which was added to the second storey of the *Fürstenhaus* directly above the entrance to the building. Finally, both as decoration and as protection from the elements, the exterior walls were given a coat of white, lime-based plaster.

With the inner courtyard being modified for the occupation of the electoral family, the outer courtyard or *Aussenhof* was also redeveloped. The location

A   COLDITZ IN THE 11TH CENTURY

This reconstruction of the original wooden defences of Colditz is based upon a similar fortification from the Rhineland dated to the year 1048. The central feature of the defence is a three-storey wooden tower or *Bergfried* (**1**) used primarily as accommodation for the garrison commander but also for storage and as a final rallying position. The outer defences consist of an embanked wooden palisade or *Burgwall* (**2**), which is punctuated by a number of firing platforms (**3**) that enable the defenders to fire upon any attacking forces. At this moment in time a number of carpenters are busily constructing a fighting platform that will eventually run the whole circuit of the defences. Cheap and easy to build, this type of fortification was common in the eastern marches of the Empire and enabled the imperial court to maintain control over large areas occupied by a potentially hostile population.

of the current youth hostel was both the accommodation of the head groom and the site of a stable for 43 horses, with a further 37 animals also being stabled along the courtyard's southern wall, and a number of kennels being added for the elector's hunting dogs. Perhaps the most dominant addition, however, was the *Pferdewaschschwemme*, or horse bath, which was built in the northern part of the courtyard.

However, Ernest was neither fated to enjoy his new possession nor to see the completion of the works that he had commissioned, for one year to the day after the signing of the 'Partition of Leipzig' he was killed in a hunting accident and it was left to his son and heir, Frederick III, to continue his father's programme of construction.

An accidental fire in 1504 caused extensive damage to both town and castle and led to a temporary cessation in building work that lasted for almost a decade, until Frederick commissioned the extension of the royal suites, chapel and buttery into a single interconnected entity, as well as the renovation of the castle stables and outer gatehouse, with the final stages of construction being completed in the years after 1519.

Events, however, would soon overtake both elector and castle when, in 1517, Martin Luther, as an objection against the Church's practice of selling 'indulgences' for the remission of sin, nailed his *95 Theses* to the door of the castle church in Wittenberg – a building that, incidentally, contained Frederick's considerable collection of religious relics and artefacts.

At the time few could have predicted the consequences of Luther's actions, but within a relatively short period others picked up his baton, and a movement

These decorative wooden panels are indicative of the craftsmanship employed in the interior decoration of the castle during the period when it served as an electoral residence. (Author)

developed in 'protestation' against what were viewed as being the excesses of the Church in Rome. Social unrest meant civil unrest, and although the Elector Frederick was to sympathize with Luther, Colditz was garrisoned with a small body of troops to protect the royal property.

As the century progressed, Colditz gradually moved on from being the shattered wreck of a medieval fortress, and emerged into the brilliance of a Renaissance Saxon court where artisans were commissioned to produce works of art to enhance the castle. Indeed, throughout the 16th century continued royal patronage saw the castle develop into a major fixture within the Saxon political landscape, in stark contrast to the austerity that would characterize the site's later use. The buildings now began to reflect their royal status – the gabled exterior of the main hall, for example, featured wrought iron decorative work surmounted by gilded flowers made from lead, whilst the guttering found expression in a number of water spouts shaped in the form of dragons and other mythical creatures. Also outside, the courtyard walls themselves were brightly painted, and now rose to a roof protected from the elements by green brickwork tiles, the whole serving to project the self-image of the ruler of one of the strongest and most prosperous of the German states. In the early 1520s, as the castle settled comfortably into its new mantle, the Elector Frederick took his plans one stage further and laid out the foundations of the *Tiergarten* which would, for a time at least, become the largest animal park in Europe. In 1525, Frederick died, and was succeeded by his brother John, who continued, with few exceptions, his sibling's secular and spiritual policies, gradually adding to the refurbishments adorning the castle overlooking the Mulde, one of which was undoubtedly the rebuilding of the outer gate with its stepped gabling.

The political upheavals of the mid-16th century saw Colditz neglected by the successive rulers, whose priorities understandably lay elsewhere, but

Once perhaps the largest menagerie in Europe, the *Tiergarten* was later used to provide the camp authorities with a secure area in which the prisoners could take their exercise, as provided for by the Geneva Convention. (Author)

in 1570 Elector August began a comprehensive programme of refurbishment. A keen huntsman, August's personal priority was that he and his companions would have somewhere to stay during their hunting trips, but as head of state, the elector was accompanied by an ever-increasing number of governmental supernumeraries, all of whom needed to be housed and fed and so what had effectively begun as a relatively minor project concluded as a major renovation of the castle. This saw the building of a small office block or *Kanzlei* to accommodate the elector's staff and provide them with a working area. As this building was effectively being used by the Saxon bureaucracy it is also often referred to as the *Beamtenhaus*, which derives from the German term for civil servants (*Beamten*). In addition to this a part of the south-western side of the outer courtyard was refurbished as a jail for offenders tried whilst the elector was resident in Colditz.

The final modification during this period was the reconstruction of the moat bridge and the main gateway to the outer courtyard above which the elector's coat of arms (twinned with those of his wife, Anne of Denmark) have been carved. With August's death on 11 February 1586, the throne passed to his sixth and eldest surviving son, Christian I, who in turn gave the title of Colditz to his wife, Sophie of Brandenburg.

LEFT
Detail of the second or inner gateway, showing the heraldic coats of arms of electoral Saxony and the kingdom of Denmark, representing the marriage of the Elector August to Anna of Denmark. (Author)

RIGHT
Erected in 1602, this close-up of the chapel entrance shows the carvings in the red porphyry gateway in exquisite detail. Originally, each of the five plinths was surmounted by a statue: the central figure of Jesus Christ being flanked by representations of Belief and Endurance, whilst the outer plinths held on one side a phoenix and on the other a pelican. (Author)

B THE HUSSITE SACK OF COLDITZ

Following the death of Jan Zizka in 1424, the Hussites decided to launch a number of pre-emptive strikes against the German states in order to deter them from taking further offensive action. In around 1431 one of these Hussite columns came upon the ill-defended town of Colditz and sacked both settlement and castle. The damage was so severe that it took a number of decades for the town to recover from its ordeal. Here we see Hussite raiders looting the buildings around the marketplace as the townspeople flee in panic, whilst above them the castle burns.

With the exception of its occupation in 1637 by Swedish forces during the Thirty Years War (1618–48) the remainder of the 17th century was a kind of swansong for Colditz, as few of the electors took an interest in the upkeep and maintenance of the castle. During the closing decade of the century, and in accordance with what had become established practice, the Elector John George IV bestowed the title upon his wife Eleonore Erdmuthe von Saxe-Eisenach upon the occasion of their wedding in 1692.

Although unprecedented urban growth during the late 1700s saw great prosperity amongst the nobility and the mercantile classes, this was not true of all social strata. Continuous warfare had resulted in large numbers of troops being demobilized with no real provision being made for their future or indeed for the dependants of those who had fallen in combat. Too poor to eke out even a basic existence, many of these former soldiers found themselves amongst the ranks of those who had already been marginalized from society. Across the German states many governments came up with a similar solution and a large number of unoccupied or decrepit castles were suitably renovated in order that these 'social undesirables' could be kept away from the public eye. In 1800 Colditz was converted into a workhouse.

As a result, the *Beamtenhaus* and certain sections of the castle were turned over to the administration of the workhouse, whilst others were converted into dormitory accommodation for the inmates, with a number of wooden galleries being built in the chapel in order that staff and patients could hear mass at the same time. The remaining rooms, where the electors once lived or entertained their guests, were simply used for storage and locked or boarded up. By 1802 this transition had been largely completed and where a multicoloured, glittering renaissance palace had once stood an empty shell now remained, the glowing artwork of earlier centuries either placed in storage, covered by wooden screens or in some instances simply covered in a thick coat of dull paint.

In 1829 the Saxon government ordered the workhouse to be closed, choosing instead to convert the castle complex into a hospital for the mentally ill, with responsibility for the Leipzig region. This was a role that it would perform almost uninterrupted for nearly a century until its eventual closure in 1924. Amongst the patients treated at Colditz were Ludwig Schumann, son of the celebrated composer Robert Schumann and Ernst Baumgarten, a pioneer of German airship technology, both of whom would die in Colditz.

Interior of the castle chapel showing the wooden galleries that were installed during the early 19th century in order that the inmates and staff could hear mass together. (Author)

After the asylum's closure, the castle remained relatively empty until the rise to power of the Nazis, when from March 1933 until late October 1934 the castle was used as one of the hundreds of camps or *Konzentrationslagern* established by Ernst Röhm's Brownshirts. Opponents of the new regime were temporarily held in 'protective custody' – a polite euphemism for the State's suspension of the inmates' basic human rights – whilst their fate was being decided. The fledgling *Schützstaffeln* (SS) were also present in Colditz at this time, but as by far the smaller of the Nazi Party's two paramilitary formations they limited their activities to the occupation of the *Schützenhaus*, headquarters of the local shooting club.

Following the execution of Röhm and the subsequent purge of the SA during Operation *Hummingbird* in June and July of 1934, Hermann Göring – as head of the German police – transferred the responsibility for the camps to Himmler's SS, and during the autumn Colditz was once again closed down and the bulk of the prisoners released.

THE LIVING SITE

Almost upon leaving the station we saw looming above us our future prison: beautiful, serene, majestic, and yet forbidding enough to make our hearts sink into our boots. It towered above us, dominating the whole village; a magnificent Castle built on the edge of a cliff... To friendly peasants and trades-people in the houses nestling beneath its shadow it may have signified protection and home, but to enemies from a distant country such a castle struck the note of doom and was a sight to make the bravest quail... The outside walls were on average seven feet thick, and the inner courtyard of the Castle was about two hundred and fifty feet above the river-level. The Castle rooms in which we were to live were about another sixty feet above the courtyard... Colditz was situated ... in the heart of the German Reich and four hundred miles from any frontier not directly under the Nazi heel. What a hope for would-be escapers!

Although these words were the initial thoughts of Captain Pat Reid upon his arrival at Colditz in November 1941, they could have reflected the opinions of any of the hundreds of captured Allied officers sent to Oflag IV-C during World War II. They also give an indirect insight into the mindset of the German high command, which constantly promoted the myth of the 'inescapable prison', and as such was determined to put the prisoners under psychological duress from the moment of their disembarkation at Colditz railway station. The rationale was that if the futility of escape was impressed on the men from the moment of their arrival, few of them would later even attempt to escape. The prisoners were deliberately led along a carefully planned route from railway station to castle, during the course of which they would be unable to avoid the looming presence of their new home.

The first close-up view that the prisoners would have had of the castle would have been the outer gatehouse with its massive wooden gates of seasoned oak reinforced with studs and cast-iron brackets. Depending upon the number of new arrivals, a door within the left-hand gate could be opened to save the guards from having to unlock and then re-lock the whole mechanism. Once through the gate the men would immediately be faced with a bridge across a dry moat leading to a second gateway that was

Memorial tablet to political prisoners who were held at Colditz in 1933–34. The inscription ends with the admonition 'They fought so that we may live'. The inverted red triangle was the badge used to identify political prisoners in Germany, and similarly the files of POWs seen as being *Deutschfeindlich* or 'anti-German' were marked with a red tab. (Author)

almost identical to the first. It was built into the base of the *Schlossturm*, the main tower, which rose almost 36m above their heads and dominated the castle's southern wall.

As this second pair of gates slammed shut behind them, the prisoners would have found themselves in the outer courtyard, which was the castle's nerve centre. Of more recent construction than the inner courtyard and measuring a mere 50m across, the focal point of the area was the *Kommandantur* or administration block, which had been rebuilt in 1864 based on the site of the eastern wing of the former stables. Overlooking a large well-kept lawn, this building was both home and workplace for many of the German staff. Like the workshops and offices that occupied the southern and south-western walls, it had been rebuilt for functionality rather than for defence.

Based on a slight incline, the remainder of the courtyard was cobbled and was punctuated by three guard positions with their red, white and black sentry boxes covering the main entrances and exits to the courtyard. The first of these the prisoners would have marched through. The second was a gated archway which, running under a parapet adjacent to the northern end of the *Kommandantur* building, provided the only road access into the

British Intelligence devised various ingenious methods to assist the prisoners in planning their escapes. Here a series of maps have been pasted inside a number of playing cards and thus concealed from prying eyes. (IWM, HU 035016)

castle. The third and final gateway that opened into this courtyard was on the north-western wall, and provided access to the inner courtyard and the prisoners' quarters. In addition to the sentries, two aerial searchlights – one on the edge of the lawn and one on the south-western wall – were deployed in order to illuminate the outer walls on the inner courtyard and give advance warning of any escape attempts from that quarter.

Passing under this third gateway, the prisoners would march through a short tunnel, passing a number of storage

The main entrance to the German *Kommandantur,* or administration block, from which Oflag IV-C was run. (Author)

Under the terms of the 3rd Geneva Convention, prisoners were entitled to receive reading material in their native language, a requirement used by British Intelligence, under the guise of various charitable agencies, as a means of smuggling maps, currency and other necessities into the camp pasted into the book covers. (IWM, HU 049542)

rooms that had been renovated specifically as cells for prisoners under *Stubenarrest* (solitary confinement). Halting in front of the *Wachhaus* (guardhouse), which had been converted from the earlier *Beamtenhaus,* and turning right they would then pass through the 'Whispering Gate', the fourth and final gateway into the inner courtyard, the heart of Colditz Castle. With its cobbled floor sloping from east to west it made for an uncomfortable surface during the inevitable (and increasingly frequent as the war continued) roll-calls, and was both physically and mentally draining for the prisoners.

Estimated by one inmate as being as big as a badly designed tennis court, this area was far older and far more cramped than the facilities enjoyed by the Germans, being built upon the foundations of the 12th-century stone fortifications. Flanked on all sides by tall buildings, which – four or five storeys high – stole much of the natural daylight,

the courtyard was a dull, dark area. Its forbidding nature was emphasized by its dilapidated state of repair and random patches of ivy snaking their way across the building façades. To quote Pat Reid once again: 'It was an unspeakably grisly place.'

Given the numerous building phases that took place during the castle's development, there are no standard measurements within the fortifications. The older, lower sections of construction, including the cellars, have been shown to have a thickness of 3.7 to 6.4m, and would have been lit by means of shafts driven through the wall that would have allowed natural daylight to filter into the rooms. Initially, these shafts would have been augmented by torches mounted in wall sconces, but as technology developed electric lighting would have been used. Although necessary, the shafts themselves created a weakness in the defences – a point of possible egress – and as such metal grilles were built into them, often some way along their length where the confined space would preclude their being cut through. By the time the castle was being used as a POW camp many of these shafts had also been glazed over from the outside.

As one ascends from the courtyard itself the storeys become more modern and their design more for accommodation or storage than for any military use. The walls become correspondingly thinner, ranging in thickness from roughly 1.2 to 2.8m, most of which are pierced for properly glazed windows, again initially augmented by torches or oil lamps and ultimately electric lighting. On the exterior facings of the courtyard buildings, many of the window openings were protected by iron grilles bolted into the stonework, which obviously precluded their use as a means of escape. In addition to this, those that were not so protected were fitted with iron bars, installed either during World War I when Colditz was first used as a POW camp or in the early 1930s when the Nazi regime used it as a camp for political prisoners.

On the right of the courtyard, facing west, stood the *Kellerhaus*, the original electoral suite and later buttery, the ground floor of which had now been divided into the prisoners' post room, where all incoming mail and food parcels would be processed by a number of 'trusted' officers under the command of a German NCO, and the sickbay, where the prisoners would be treated by their own medical officers under the nominal command of the German medical officer. Overall supervision of this part of the castle was in the hands of Stabsfeldwebel Gephard, whom the prisoners had christened with the nickname 'Mussolini'. His office directly opposite the sickbay was

The inner courtyard, looking towards the prisoners' kitchen area. The entrance to the Belgian, Dutch and Polish quarters was via the doorway in the centre of the photograph. (Author)

erroneously believed by the Germans to be one of the most secure locations within the castle because of a unique and expensive lock that had been fitted to the door. In time, the lock would be picked and a group of prisoners would use the office as the launching-off point for an escape attempt. Finally, a flight of stairs led down from the entrance of the building to the Germans' wine cellar, a locked vault that would play a pivotal part in the excavation of the French tunnel later known as 'Le Métro'. Occupied by officers of the French contingent, the upper floors were reached through the spiral stairwell in the clock tower joining the *Kellerhaus* to the chapel, a building that had remained largely unchanged since its initial completion, but the external glory of which had been tarnished somewhat by the removal of a number of statues from its carved porphyry entrance.

The eastern side of the courtyard was occupied by the *Fürstenhaus*, the former electoral residence which was home to the Anglo-Commonwealth officers on the upper left-hand side of the building and to the Dutch, Poles and Belgians on the right. On the ground floor was a small surgery where the town dentist could perform minor procedures on the prisoners; more complicated treatments would be conducted at the dental practice in town. Later during the war, the ground floor was used to house the *Prominenten*, a group of prisoners of different nationalities who, by virtue of their military rank or familial connections, the German government had decided had a potential hostage value.

The southern side of the courtyard contained the prisoners' canteen and kitchens, which were originally separated from each other but eventually the open area between them was roofed over to provide a better use of the available space. The south-eastern corner was occupied by a wooden shed that was used for delousing and behind this a stairwell led into the largest of the interior buildings, the *Saalhaus* or Great Hall, where the Saxon electors had previously entertained their guests. Divided into two sections, the southern part of the building was used to quarter the senior Allied officers and their orderlies, whilst the ground floor of the northern part had been refurbished as the prisoners' main bathing area. Finally the third floor of the building, reached by another spiral staircase, was home to the camp theatre.

C   NEXT PAGE: AN OVERHEAD VIEW OF COLDITZ

The French quarters were in the *Kellerhaus*, above the sickbay, whilst those of the British, Dutch, Belgians and Poles were in the *Fürstenhaus* above the dental surgery.

Inset one – Here Squadron Leader Brian Paddon attempts to return a watch belonging to a young German woman. Unknown to Paddon the 'woman' was in fact a French officer in disguise and this misplaced chivalry ultimately led to the Frenchman's recapture.

Inset two – Here Lieutenant 'Tony' Luteijn, disguised as a German captain, remonstrates with a hapless sentry whilst an anxious Airey Neave looks on. Both men were to successfully make their way to freedom, Neave being the first British officer to do so.

Key:
1. German courtyard
2. Prisoners' courtyard
3. *Kommandantur*
4. Outer gateway
5. Main gateway
6. Whispering Gate
7. Guardhouse
8. German mess
9. Chapel
10. *Prominenten* quarters
11. Sickbay
12. Cells
13. Canteen
14. Kitchen
15. German kitchen
16. Coal bunker
17. Machine-gun position
18. Watchtower
19. Catwalk
20. Park
21. Senior officers' quarters

Security in the inner courtyard was provided by two sentries, one deployed at the delousing sheds and the other at the entrance to the British quarters, who were supported by the *Rollkommando* or 'riot squad' based in the Wachhaus. In addition, an aerial spotlight was deployed to cover the eastern side of the courtyard based around the *Fürstenhaus* and the British quarters.

Outside of the main prison complex, the clifftop escarpment was secured within a thick belt of barbed-wire fencing up to 3.6m in height, through which there was only one exit – a gated catwalk along the eastern flank of the castle overlooking the *Tiergarten*. This perimeter was manned by a further 11 sentries, again with a number of searchlights to illuminate the walls and deter potential escapers. There were eight men and four lamps on the western perimeter, one man and two lamps to the north and two men with three searchlights covering the east. In addition to these precautions, the relatively open north-western side of the castle was also covered by a wooden guard tower known as the '*Pagoda*' and a machine-gun post built on top of the round tower that stood at the head of the western terrace.

Finally, the hillside approaches to the *Tiergarten* were also strewn with lengths of barbed wire to prevent the prisoners from escaping down the slopes, and after the initial escapes the Germans constructed a barbed-wire enclosure in which the prisoners would have to conduct their exercise periods.

THE SITE IN WAR

Despite the departure of the political internees in 1934, Colditz was not fated to remain empty for long, being occupied shortly afterwards by labourers of the Reich Labour Service. This had been formed that year in an effort to combat unemployment and its members were used by the government as an unpaid workforce on various civil engineering projects.

The German invasion of Poland and the outbreak of World War II in September 1939 meant that facilities needed to be prepared for containing an inevitable influx of prisoners of war and, like many castles throughout Germany, Colditz was pressed into service as a POW camp or *Kriegsgefangenenlager*. The reason for this was quite simple in that although their original purpose had been to keep people out, with minimal effort these fortresses could be suitably upgraded in order to keep people in.

Accordingly, on October 31, on the orders of the commanding officer of Wehrkreis IV based in Dresden, Colditz was given the official title 'Offizierslager IV-C', or as it is more commonly referred to: 'Oflag IV-C'. The title comprises three elements standard throughout the camp system: the title '*Offizierslager*' refers to the fact that this was a camp for captured officers, the Roman numeral 'IV' denotes the responsible *Wehrkreis* (military district) and the suffix 'C' indicates that the camp is the third in the sequential list of camps within the district, the others in this case being the castles of Hohnstein (IV-A), Königstein (IV-B) and Elsterhorst (IV-D).

In addition to the above, Colditz was initially given a secondary designation of '*Durchgangslager*', indicating that the camp was primarily intended for use as a transit camp for the collection and processing of prisoners before their transfer to other facilities. In November 1940, however, this designation was changed to '*Straflager*' (punishment camp), whereby problematic prisoners from all over Germany and occupied Europe were sent in order that they could be concentrated in a single location in an attempt

Contemporary aerial view of Colditz, taken from the south-west. The terraces and dry moat can be clearly distinguished in the foreground to the right. (IWM, HU 049551). (Author)

to ease the administrative strain on the system. The final change came in 1943 when an influx of political or '*Deutschfeindlich*' (anti-German) prisoners caused it to be reclassified as a '*Sonderlager*' (special camp), a role it fulfilled until its liberation by American forces in April 1945.

From the outset, the administration of Colditz was divided into two separate entities. Resident in the castle was the *Lagerkommandant* (camp commander) – generally an officer of field rank – who, assisted by a *Vizekommandant* (vice-commander) and their respective adjutants, oversaw the running of the camp and its immediate staff, both military personnel and civilian contract workers. Supporting the administrative staff was a company of security troops tasked with providing the *Kommandant* with sufficient manpower to man the various guard posts and also to serve as escorts during the transportation of prisoners. Initially this duty was undertaken by 4. Kompanie of Landesschützenbataillon 395 under the command of Hauptmann Georg Thomann. Three platoons of troops were based within the castle itself – the first in the *Saalhaus* underneath the Allied senior officers' quarters and the remaining two in the former hospital building overlooking the castle park, and it is presumed that the remaining platoon oversaw security at the *Schützenhaus* after it had been pressed into service as a satellite of the main camp.

Immediately below the *Kommandant* and his deputy came a number of officers, each supported by a cadre of senior NCOs, whose duties brought them into the closest and most direct contact with the prisoners. The first, and arguably the most important of these, were the *Lageroffiziere* (camp officers), whose remit included the responsibility for conducting the daily roll-calls (*Appelle*), manning the various guard posts throughout the castle, and maintaining a number of guard patrols. Generally there were four such officers, whose titles were suffixed by the numbers 1–4, with 'LO1' being the most senior of the quartet. Owing to manpower shortages or staff reassignments the actual number of such officers on duty at Colditz often fluctuated during the course of the war.

For both propaganda and training purposes, all escape attempts were recorded and displayed within the castle's 'Escape Museum', exhibits from which were later displayed at a number of symposia attended by security officers from a number of camps. (Author)

LEFT
In this re-enactment of a failed escape attempt, the Dutch escape officer Machiel van den Heuvel is supported by two British officers as he emerges from a hole dug into the cell wall. (IWM, HU 049540).

RIGHT
Oberst Max Schmidt, first *Kommandant* of Oflag IV-C, Colditz. (IWM, HU 086543)

Colditz during World War II

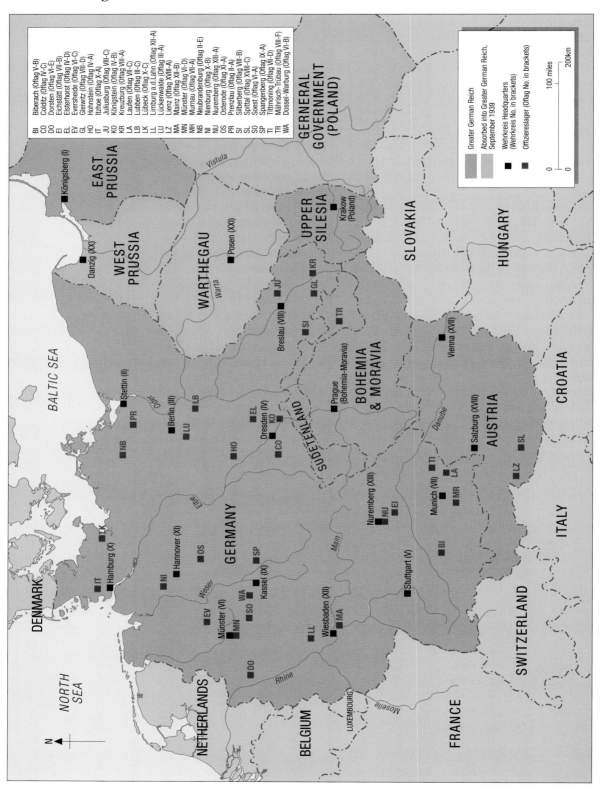

BI Biberach (Oflag V-B)
CO Colditz (Oflag IV-C)
DO Dorsten (Oflag VI-E)
EI Eichstätt (Oflag VII-B)
EL Elsterhorst (Oflag IV-D)
EV Eversheide (Oflag VI-C)
GL Gleiwitz (Oflag VIII-D)
HO Hohnstein (Oflag IV-A)
IT Itzhoe (Oflag X-A)
JU Juliusburg (Oflag VIII-C)
KO Königstein (Oflag IV-B)
KR Kreuzburg (Oflag VIII-A)
LA Laufen (Oflag VII-C)
LB Lubben (Oflag III-C)
LK Lübeck (Oflag X-C)
LL Limburg a.d.Lahn (Oflag XII-A)
LU Luckenwalde (Oflag III-A)
LZ Lienz (Oflag XIII-A)
MA Mainz (Oflag XII-B)
MN Münster (Oflag VI-D)
MR Murnau (Oflag VII-A)
NB Neubrandenburg (Oflag II-E)
NI Nienburg (Oflag X-D)
NU Nuremberg (Oflag XIII-A)
OS Osterode (Oflag XI-A)
PR Prenzlau (Oflag II-A)
SI Silberberg (Oflag VIII-B)
SL Spittal (Oflag XVIII-C)
SO Soest (Oflag VI-A)
SP Spangenberg (Oflag IX-A)
TI Tittmoning (Oflag VII-D)
TR Mährisch-Trübau (Oflag VIII-F)
WA Dossel-Warburg (Oflag VI-B)

EAST PRUSSIA

WEST PRUSSIA

WARTHEGAU

UPPER SILESIA

GERNERAL GOVERNMENT (POLAND)

SLOVAKIA

HUNGARY

Greater German Reich

Absorbed into Greater German Reich, September 1939

■ Wehrkreis Headquarters (Wehrkreis No. in brackets)

■ Offizierslager (Oflag No. in brackets)

0   100 miles
0   200km

Königsberg (I)

Danzig (XX)

Posen (XXI)

Krakow (Poland)

Vistula

Warta

BALTIC SEA

Stettin (II)

PR

NB

Berlin (III)

LU

LB

JU

GL KR

Breslau (VIII)

SI

TR

Vienna (XVII)

BOHEMIA & MORAVIA

AUSTRIA

CROATIA

EL

KO

Dresden (IV)

CO

HO

Prague (Bohemia-Moravia)

Salzburg (XVIII)

SL

LZ

SUDETENLAND

Oder

Elbe

Danube

GERMANY

Hamburg (X)

LK

IT

Hannover (XI)

OS

NI

EV

MN WA

SO

Kassel (IX)

SP

DO

Wiesbaden (XII)

LL MA

Stuttgart (V)

Nuremberg (XIII)

NU

EI

BI

Munich (VII)

TI

LA

MR

Weser

Main

Rhine

Moselle

NORTH SEA

DENMARK

NETHERLANDS

BELGIUM

LUXEMBOURG

FRANCE

SWITZERLAND

ITALY

N

Next in line, and with duties that both supported and partially overlapped those of the *Lageroffiziere*, came the *Abwehroffizier* (security officer) whose principal task was to counter any escape attempts by the prisoners. The importance of this role can best be exemplified by the fact that late in the war, the Germans held a number of symposia attended by security officers delegated from various camps, during which Allied escape attempts (both successful and unsuccessful) were analysed and methods of detection and prevention discussed and developed.

Finally there came the officer in charge of the guard-dog detachment, which was concerned with the provision of canine support for the camp. In effect, this could range from the presence of guard dogs during roll-calls, organizing dog patrols around the castle and its grounds or the provision of dogs as back-up for 'snap' raids against suspected escape attempts.

The remainder of the camp's staff were drawn from the ranks of the *Wehrmachtsbeamten* – in effect a military civil service – who were primarily concerned with the camp administration on a day-to-day basis. As well as providing the secretarial staff, their numbers also included a legal officer (*Rechtsoffizier*), paymaster (*Stabszahlmeister*), camp doctor (*Stabsarzt*) and a number of translators (*Übersetzer*).

In addition to the above, two local civilians were also co-opted onto the castle staff on an ad hoc basis. These were Johannes Lange, a local photographer who was called upon to document the history of the camp, and the town's dentist, who was provided with basic facilities within the castle to treat the prisoners' teeth.

Upon his appointment in October 1939, the initial task that faced the first *Kommandant* of Colditz – Oberst Max Schmidt – was how to divide up the camp between prisoners and guards. Luckily for him, the actual layout of the castle lent itself to a ready solution: the outer courtyard and all of the buildings that opened onto it would be reserved for the camp administration

Situated next to the entrance of the inner courtyard, the *Beamtenhaus* was used by the Germans as the principal guardhouse in Colditz. It now houses the castle museum. (Author)

offices whilst the inner courtyard and, in effect, the entire northern half of the castle would be used to house the prisoners. This area was then divided up not only into living quarters for the various nationalities who would be incarcerated in Colditz, but also into the facilities to which they were entitled under the Geneva Convention. As they would in theory be easier to monitor, Schmidt elected to allocate the ground floor of many of the buildings of the inner courtyard for this latter purpose, with the upper stories reserved for prisoner accommodation.

With both courtyards thus partitioned, Schmidt then ordered the construction of a barbed-wire fence encompassing the exterior of the inner courtyard complex and continuing south along the side of the park, thereby encircling the prisoners with a second line of obstacles that would have to be negotiated before any escape attempt could be made. Finally, a number of fixed sentry positions were established, complemented by a number of roving patrols, which provided a third – human – barrier to any escape attempts.

The first POWs arrive

For the first year of the war, Colditz remained simply a transit camp, but on 1 November 1940 this designation was changed with the arrival of a number of Polish prisoners sent from the nearby Oflag IV-A, Hohnstein, and Oflag VIII-B, Silberberg, in Lower Silesia. Thus Schmidt, having reorganized the layout of the castle complex, now had to address the question of the reception of the prisoners themselves.

Colditz Castle as seen from the *Bahnhofsvorplatz* outside the train station. This was the assembly point for all prisoners whether arriving or departing Colditz, and in all cases this perspective would have been their lasting view of the castle. (Author)

Given its geographical location, it was decided early on that where possible the transfer of prisoners to Colditz would take place by rail, a reasonable decision to make given that prisoners would eventually be sent to Oflag IV-C not in ones or twos but in their tens and hundreds. This worked to the Germans' psychological advantage in that as soon as the new arrivals were assembled in the *Bahnhofsvorplatz* – the small square in front of the railway station – the first thing that they would see would be the castle itself, rising from its rocky eyrie on the opposite side of the Mulde. Here, and once their travel papers were found to be correct, the prisoners would be signed over to the commander of a guard detachment from the castle who, after checking the number of the new arrivals against a security list, would then order his men to begin the mile-long journey back to the camp.

From the railway station the column would march eastwards along Brückenstrasse, crossing the Mulde via the Adolf Hitler Brücke (Adolf Hitler Bridge) where, with the castle looming always above them and never completely out of view, they would continue their 'Via Dolorosa' along the cobbled Badergasse before ascending steeply into the town square from which a small twisting stairway led to the outer gatehouse. It was a route designed to capitalize on the prisoners' hunger and fatigue, to demoralize them with both the arduous nature of the ascent, and indeed with the omnipresent nature of the complex itself, for at no stage during the march was the castle ever out of the prisoners' sight.

Once inside the castle, the prisoners and their escort would be met by a small party under the command of the duty officer, who would bring them into one of the rooms off the *Kommandantur* and there 'process' the new arrivals, a procedure which invariably meant cross-checking each individual's papers firstly against their travel orders and then against the camp records

New arrivals – a contingent of French prisoners being marched under escort across the Adolf Hitler Brücke en route to Colditz. (Australian War Memorial, Canberra – P01608-001)

French prisoners assemble in the courtyard for a Bastille Day parade. The fact that the area is almost full in this photograph illustrates how cramped the situation would be when the other Allied contingents were also present in the courtyard for one of the regular roll-calls. (Australian War Memorial, Canberra – P01608-006).

themselves. After this was done the prisoner was given a copy of form M/0162 upon which was listed, in both German and the prisoner's native language, those articles that the camp authorities deemed to be contraband. These included hard currency, civilian clothing, compasses, maps, cameras etc. – in effect anything that it was felt could be used in planning and executing an escape. The prisoner was then asked if he understood the restrictions on the list and invited to hand over any such items in his possession with the caveat that he would be punished should he decline and any of the listed items be subsequently found on his person. Items thus surrendered were then receipted and signed for and a copy given to the prisoner, who would at this stage, then be subjected to a search. In normal circumstances, a simple body search would be performed, but dependent on the notes in the individual's prison file it could then be extended to a 'strip' or 'full cavity' search conducted by a medical officer.

Given the fact that, as a *Sonderlager*, Colditz was to be home to the most troublesome of the Allied POWs in German hands, the nature of their

D   THE ARRIVAL OF THE LAUFEN SIX

Suitably unimpressed by their new surroundings, here we see Capt. Reid (**1**), Capt. Barry (**2**), Lt. Allan (**3**), Capt. Howe (**4**), Capt. Elliott (**5**) and Capt. Lockwood (**6**) looking on disinterestedly whilst the commander of the guard detachment from the castle signs their transfer papers to confirm their arrival at Colditz. These officers would eventually play a central role in most of the British escape attempts from the castle. Of the six, only Reid would make a successful 'home run', whilst Elliott would be repatriated as a result of a faked medical condition. The remaining members of the Laufen Six would spend the rest of the war as prisoners at Colditz.

The arrival of the Laufen Six

reception was specifically orchestrated as a form of psychological warfare, in order to immediately establish the Germans' superiority and place the prisoners under mental pressure. Perhaps the worst aspect of this treatment surfaced once their records had been checked and any body search conducted. On their arrival at Colditz – and possibly owing to their being the first prisoners sent to Oflag IV-C – the Poles were addressed personally by Kommandant Schmidt, his words echoing what was to become official German policy with regard to Polish prisoners:

> According to the dispositions set out in the Geneva Convention for the treatment of prisoners of war, the Armed Forces High Command has instituted this Special Prisoner of War Camp – Oflag IV-C Colditz – into which you Poles have been admitted as a special case. Poland no longer exists and it is only due to the magnanimity of our Führer that you are benefiting temporarily from the privileges such as will be accorded to prisoners of war of the other belligerent powers who will be held at the camp. You should be grateful to Adolf Hitler who, by his decision, has favoured you. You, who in 1939 by your stupid obstinacy were responsible for starting this war.

As Schmidt spoke, his captive audience looked on incredulously, unable to believe their ears. Unwilling to accept Schmidt's proclamation, the Poles unanimously decided to make life as difficult as possible for their captors by planning a campaign of passive resistance, their main weapon being to deny the Germans the respect that they themselves should have received as a signatory to the Geneva Convention. As an example, officers would refuse to salute their German counterparts, preferring to be 'court-martialled' by the Germans and spend time in solitary confinement, or accept any other punishment levied.

As a result, the Poles did not immediately set their minds to escape, but decided rather to discover everything they could about their prison, and as night fell and the dormitory lights went out all over Colditz they began their nocturnal excursions, checking locks, exploring rooms and passageways until

LEFT
Senior Allied officers pose in front of the chapel entrance, amongst them Admiral Józef Unrug (third from left) and Colonel David Stayner (third from right). (IWM, HU 020269)

RIGHT
Photograph from the file of Capt. Pat Reid, taken during his captivity at Laufen (Oflag VII-C). (IWM, HU 049547)

OFLAG VIIC357

eventually they had a better knowledge of the buildings surrounding the inner courtyard than did their captors, and by the time that prisoners from other Allied nations began to arrive at the castle, there were few rooms to which they had not gained access and even fewer locks that had remained unpicked in the face of a sustained and dedicated Polish assault.

Five days after the Poles' arrival in the castle, the first Commonwealth prisoners, all Canadians serving with the RAF, arrived at Colditz from Oflag IX-A/H Burg Spangenberg near Kassel. They were Flying Officers Donald Middleton, Keith Milne and Howard Wardle, who were subsequently joined by six British officers on 7 November. Known as the 'Laufen Six' from their previous camp (Oflag VII-C at Laufen in Upper Bavaria) these men – Captains Rupert Barry, Harry Elliott, Richard Howe MC, Kenneth Lockwood and Pat Reid, and Lieutenant Anthony 'Peter' Allan – would all play leading roles in the organization of many of the future British escape attempts.

As 1940 drew to a close and the number of prisoners held in Colditz steadily increased, the cosmopolitan nature of the camp was accentuated by the arrival of 12 Belgian and 50 French officers. Amongst the new inmates however, was a civilian prisoner, Howard Gee, who had been captured by the Germans in Norway after having served as a volunteer in the Finnish army during the Winter War against Russia. Unsure of what to do with him, his captors had quite simply, and for want of a better alternative, sent him to Colditz.

At the beginning of 1941 increasing numbers of Allied officers were to find themselves disembarking at Colditz railway station, prior to their arrival at the castle. In February 1941, the French General Le Bleu arrived at the head of a further contingent of 200 men, of whom some 140 had been moved to the camp on account of their overt *Deutschfeindlichkeit* whereas the remainder were mainly officers of Jewish origin.

Although Hitler's policy towards the Jews had not, as yet, openly manifested itself throughout occupied Europe, Colditz was now beset by a wave of anti-Semitism from within as a number of French officers turned on their erstwhile comrades-in-arms, petitioning Kommandant Schmidt to forcibly segregate the French contingent into Jews and Gentiles. Although many felt this to be unfair, the 'official' British position as decided by Lieutenant-Colonel Guy German, the senior British officer, was that it was a private matter for the French and that the British should not become involved. Needless to say this policy was not strictly adhered to, and in time a number of officers ignored the segregation and made contact with the new prisoners, some of whom were actually scions of some of France's most prominent families such as Robert Blum (son of a former Prime Minister of France) and Élie de Rothschild, a member of the banking dynasty.

In his later account of his experiences, Lieutenant Airey Neave, one of the officers who decided to flout Lt. Col. German's recommendations, would write: 'The camp was divided as to the wisdom and fairness of this anti-Semitism, for many of the French officers were suspected of sharing the defeatist sentiments of Vichy. Nevertheless, it was difficult to understand why they should respond to racial discrimination, and I never quite fathomed the psychology of this incident... Few of them (the Jews) were keen escapers, but the behaviour of their fellow officers in a fascist prison camp seemed to me to be outrageous'.

On 27 March 1941, the first transfer of prisoners away from Colditz began when 27 Polish officers were ordered to collect

Forged travel permit issued to Capt. Rupert Barry, listing him as a Belgian-born foreign worker. The photograph was taken in front of the chapel in the prisoner's courtyard using a home-made camera. (IWM, HU 035029)

A column of Polish prisoners seen here leaving Colditz via the outer gate. (Author)

their belongings and assemble in the inner courtyard, prior to their transportation to Oflag VII-B at Eichstätt. Although the number of officers involved was minor in relation to the total number of Poles then held in the castle, the fact that many of them had been particularly troublesome to their captors gave many reason to believe that the selection process was not as random as it had at first seemed, and that their ranks had been infiltrated by at least one informer. This suspicion was to be well founded as, long after the event, it was discovered that the Poles' canteen officer had indeed been working under duress for the Germans, due to the presence of his surviving family in occupied Warsaw.

First escape attempts

It can only be assumed that the implied threat of infiltration as much as any perceived national traits had discouraged the various nationalities from mutual cooperation. Whilst the French commenced digging a tunnel in the clock tower adjacent to their quarters, both the British and Polish contingents began preparing their own escape attempts. The British began the construction of a tunnel underneath the prisoners' canteen, which it was hoped would facilitate the escape of the whole British and Commonwealth contingent. This isolationism, however, was short-lived as the German guards soon detected the French excavations and narrowly failed to uncover the British tunnel. As a result, Kommandant Schmidt subsequently ordering that all doors leading into the clock tower from the upper dormitories be bricked up. Undeterred by this unexpected success on the part of their captors, the French simply waited until the furore had died down and made a second entrance, this time in the top of the tower where the clock mechanism was housed, which allowed them to lower men down into the base of the tower in order to continue digging and enlarge the original excavation.

By now convinced that mutual cooperation was the only way to guarantee success, each senior officer agreed to appoint one of his subordinates as 'escape officer', a man whose primary task would be to review, approve and support any proposed escape attempts by his fellow nationals. His secondary task, which was arguably just as important, was to liaise with his fellow escape officers to ensure that there would not be any conflict in proposed plans. Again, and with due attention to security, only individual escape officers themselves would be made aware of their allies' plans unless, of course, the projected attempt was to be made jointly by officers of different nationalities. As a final measure, these individuals were forbidden from taking part in any escape attempt whilst serving in this role.

Four thwarted escape attempts during the spring of 1941 seemed to convince the camp authorities that, perched upon its rocky prominence, Colditz was indeed escape-proof. However, the first chink in the seemingly impenetrable German armour was not long in coming when, on 11 April, French officer Lieutenant Alain Le Ray of the 159e Régiment d'Infanterie Alpine decided to attempt a 'snap' escape – in other words an attempt relying

LEFT
Lieutenant Alain Le Ray of the Chasseurs Alpins, the first Allied officer to escape successfully from Colditz and make a 'home run'. (Courtesy of the IWM, HU 086545)

RIGHT
Sentry duty in winter. Note the position of the searchlight to cover the castle walls. To the rear of the image is the Hainberg. (IWM, HU 086541)

The 2m-high wall surrounding the park proved to be both a deterrent and a chink in the armour of the German measures to prevent prisoners from escaping Colditz. After the initial escapes from the park, it was supplemented by the construction of a barbed-wire enclosure, within which the prisoners had their exercise periods. (Author)

on little or no forward planning. Deciding that his best chance of success would occur outside of the main castle buildings, Le Ray had, for several weeks, studied the routine of the guards escorting the prisoners down to the castle park for their exercise periods. Eventually he discovered a crucial oversight on the part of the Germans – a bend in the pathway which meant that for a matter of seconds part of the group would be out of sight of their escorts, and this would be his opening.

The overriding question now was whether these few seconds would be enough for him to make his attempt. Believing them sufficient, Le Ray began to develop his plans, confiding only in two of his fellow officers, Lieutenants André Tournon and Pierre Mairesse Lebrun. The escape in itself was simple; when out of sight of the guards, Le Ray hid in the undergrowth and waited until the party had returned to the castle before taking shelter in the cellar of a ruined summerhouse where he waited until nightfall. Later, under cover of darkness, he climbed over the stone park wall and then simply walked to Colditz railway station where he boarded the first of a number of trains that took him eventually to Switzerland and freedom. After successfully crossing into neutral territory, he eventually made his way back to unoccupied France.

From the prisoners' perspective, this first successful escape (or 'home run' as they later became known) underlined the unwritten rule that the first duty of a captured officer was to escape, but it also served notice to their German captors that Colditz was not as secure as they or their propagandists would have liked to have believed. As a result, Oberst Schmidt ordered an immediate tightening of the security regime: additional, random roll-calls were now to be added to the daily timetable, the frequency of security patrols was increased, barbed-wire fences were both reinforced and heightened, and, crucially, searchlights were installed in the outer castle yards where they were positioned to play upon the castle walls and courtyard interiors, where they could immediately illuminate any prisoners attempting to escape.

The first British escape attempt was made on 10 May when a group of French labourers came to the castle in order to collect a number of straw mattresses. The diminutive Lt. 'Peter' Allan was sewn into one of them before it was thrown into the back of a truck for transport into town. After a short journey, the truck stopped and the mattresses were then unloaded into an old house for storage. Once the labourers had left, Allan emerged from his concealment dressed in shorts, knee socks and a casual jacket – an improvised outfit that he hoped would allow him to pass as a member of the *Hitler Jugend* (Hitler Youth). A fluent German speaker, Allan initially travelled westwards towards Stuttgart, from where he was offered a lift by a senior SS

In this staged reconstruction a German guard is seen studying the rope used by Lts. Chmiel and Surmanowicz in their escape attempt of 12 May 1941. The escape was thwarted because of the noise made by Chmiel's mountaineering boots as the men abseiled down the guardhouse wall, which woke the duty officer and led him to call out the guard. (Australian War Memorial, Canberra – P01608-010)

officer. After a nerve-wracking journey, during which the slightest error would have meant recapture, he reached the Austrian capital of Vienna.

With little money and relying on the fact that his stepmother was an American citizen, Allan decided to approach the United States Consulate in the hope that he would be able to obtain help and eventually be repatriated. But conscious of the delicate political situation in Europe and possibly fearing that Allan was an *agent provocateur*, the Americans declined to help the fugitive. Allan, both starving and exhausted by his travails, turned himself in at a local police station and was returned to Colditz on 31 May where the *Kommandant* immediately sentenced him to three months' solitary confinement.

Any euphoria that the prisoners had felt on Allan's escape was quickly tempered two days later by the capture of two Poles – Lieutenants Mietek Chmiel and Miki Surmanowicz – as they clambered down one of the outside walls using a rope made from prison bed sheets. There was also the recapture on 20 May of their countryman, Lieutenant Just, after his third escape attempt in as many weeks, this time from the hospital at Villingen where he had been sent for treatment following his earlier recapture whilst trying to swim across the Rhine near Basel on the Swiss–German border.

Flying Officer Norman Forbes. One of the 'unsung heroes' of Colditz, Forbes' background in civil engineering was crucial in a number British escape attempts. (Justin Forbes)

Two weeks later, a dozen Anglo-Polish officers attempted to escape via the British tunnel under the prisoners' canteen. Overseen by Capt. Pat Reid and a new arrival, Flight Lieutenant Norman Forbes – both of whom had a background in civil engineering – nothing was left to chance and an attempt was made to bribe one of the guards by offering him several hundred Reichsmarks to be elsewhere when the escapers emerged from the tunnel. Although the bribe was a considerable one, representing both the pooling of considerable resources and several weeks' salary for the guard, the sentry reported the attempted bribe to Hauptmann Priem, the LO1, who ordered him to accept the money and say nothing, suggesting in effect that he would be a willing party to the British overtures.

On the night of 29 May, Reid – the first in a small column of would-be escapers – left the tunnel and emerged into a circle of waiting guards. Realizing that the prisoners had been double-crossed, he immediately called out a warning to the men waiting behind, but it was useless as a second group of guards had already been sent to block the tunnel entrance. All told, 11 British and two Polish officers were captured, including Lt. Col. German and the remaining members of the Laufen Six. As a result of this coup Kommandant Schmidt saw fit to overlook any misconduct on the part of the guard, and instead allowed him not only to keep 100 Reichsmarks from the attempted bribe but also awarded him discretionary leave and endorsed a citation awarding him the *Wehrverdienstkreuz II* (War Service Cross 2nd Class).

This unlooked-for success notwithstanding, German pride was soon destined to take another dent when a second French officer, Lieutenant René Collin – in an almost carbon copy of Le Ray's attempt – again successfully used the park as an avenue of escape. With this second French 'home run', and ever mindful of the terms of the Geneva Convention, Kommandant Schmidt belatedly attempted to close this apparent gap in the castle's defences by ordering the construction of a wired-off area within the park, an enclosure in which all future exercise periods would be held under close observation by the guards. It was, he felt, the perfect solution to the problem as despite these new measures the prisoners could in no way complain that their rights were being infringed.

This increased security outside the main facility was in no way reflected by any immediate change in the day-to-day running of the camp. The prisoners took great advantage of the latitude governing the receipt of parcels and many arranged for their loved ones to send them contraband goods in order to facilitate an escape attempt. On 25 June, a party of British prisoners returning from their exercise period saw a young German woman walking along the path leading up to the German courtyard, and expressed their appreciation of her presence with a chorus of whistles and catcalls. One of the officers – Squadron Leader Brian Paddon – noticing that her watch had fallen to the ground, picked it up and called out her to stop. The young woman carried on walking and Paddon started to give chase, but his objective continued walking away. In order that his actions should not be misconstrued, Paddon then gave the watch to the nearest guard who promptly ran after the girl. As soon as the soldier drew level with her, it became quickly apparent that 'she' was in fact a 'he'. It was Lieutenant Boulé, a French officer whose wife had sent him various articles of female clothing, make-up and a long blonde wig over time, thus enabling him to put together a realistic disguise, which, but for a cruel twist of fate, might have seen him safely out of the castle.

Although Boulé's near success can be seen as having demonstrated the advantage of an elaborate disguise, Lt. Pierre Mairesse Lebrun, one of his fellow officers, was soon to show the benefits of a more 'minimalist' approach. Over several days, and having established a personal regimen in which he would run for an hour and then spend the rest of his exercise period sunbathing whilst surreptitiously observing the guard detail, Lebrun made his attempt on the afternoon of 2 July, when he began jogging around the perimeter fence with Lieutenant Pierre Odry. On their final lap, and as they approached a pre-arranged point, Odry sprinted ahead and then turned, facing Lebrun with his hands clasped together. Continuing his run, Lebrun leapt into Odry's hands and vaulted over the 2.4m-high wire fence. Ignoring cries for him to halt, and furiously zigzagging to avoid the guards' fire, Lebrun waited until the Germans were forced to reload and then used these precious seconds to scale the park wall.

With a rainstorm helping to deter the German pursuit and wearing nothing but a sleeveless leather tunic, vest, shorts

Prisoners often 'pooled' the contents of their Red Cross parcels in order to supply escapers with adequate sustenance whilst 'on the run'. German staff are here seen posing with foodstuffs stockpiled for use in the thwarted 'toilet escape'. (IWM, HU 049534)

Photograph from the file of Lt. Pierre Mairesse Lebrun, taken during his captivity at Dössel-Warburg (Oflag VI-B). (IWM, HU 086547)

OFLAG VI B 592

and sports shoes, Lebrun walked south-west to the town of Zwickau. There, and fearing a resumption of the chase when the weather cleared, he stole an unattended bicycle and continued south-west with the intent of reaching the Swiss border, deflecting close attention from his clothing and bad German by cheerfully declaring to inquisitive locals that he was an Italian officer on leave from the front who had decided to spend his time touring the land of his homeland's 'Great Ally'.

After eight days' travel, as Lebrun neared the Swiss border disaster struck. The bicycle that had faithfully carried him to the brink of safety collapsed and, taking the bicycle pump with him, he was forced to continue on foot. Before he could cross over into Switzerland however, fate had one more card to play in the form of a local policeman out on a routine patrol. Fearing capture should he be spotted, Lebrun waited until the German was almost on top of him and then attacked the policeman with the only weapon to hand – the bicycle pump. As his hapless victim slumped bleeding to the ground Lebrun sprinted for the border and freedom. He was the third French officer to successfully escape from Colditz and make a 'home run'.

It was about this time that the Germans established a formal satellite of the main camp at the *Schützenhaus*, and soon a number of French officers of White Russian origin were transferred there in the hope that a less strict regime might make them susceptible to blandishments about their joining the Germans in a 'crusade against World Bolshevism'. On 17–18 July the camp received a visit from the Orthodox Bishop of Dresden accompanied by members of the choir of the Church of St Simeon Stylites. Using the celebrations as a cover, Lt. Théodore Tatistcheff was able make his escape, the fourth French officer to do so, eventually reaching safety in Lyons after narrowly escaping the clutches of the Gestapo in occupied Paris.

On 24 July 1941, the first Dutch prisoners arrived at Colditz – a detachment of 68 officers drawn from both the Dutch Home Forces and the Dutch East Indies Army (Koninklijk Nederlands-Indisch Leger) elements of which had been transferred to Europe for home defence at the beginning of hostilities in 1939. The collapse of the outnumbered and outgunned Dutch forces during the German invasion of May 1940 had induced the Germans to underestimate their opponents, and so, as a propaganda exercise, captured officers were subsequently offered their freedom if they would agree to sign a parole to the effect that they would no longer bear arms against Germany. Although many officers of the Home Army acceded to German inducements and signed the parole, almost all those of the Koninklijk Nederlands-Indisch Leger refused to sign the document, viewing it as being tantamount to breaking their oath of loyalty to their sovereign, and as a consequence were soon marching eastwards into captivity.

By this stage there were now over 500 men being held captive in Colditz and whilst their nationalities were diverse (35 Belgians, 50 British and Commonwealth, 68 Dutch, 200 French, 150 Polish and 2 Yugoslavs), equally so were the talents that they brought to what some would soon refer to as 'The Bad Boys Club', or even more simply 'The Escape Academy'. Artists, engineers, linguists, locksmiths, tailors – all of these, and more, would play their part in disproving German claims that Colditz, Oflag IV-C, was escape-proof.

As soon as they had settled in to their new quarters, the Dutch began to turn their minds to escape and like the French before them they saw exercise periods as the perfect cover under which to make the attempt. In the park there was a manhole cover which gave access to the drains, and, during a number of 'international' football matches between the various contingents, the Dutch used the crowds to obscure their replacement of the securing bolt with an identical copy made from glass and wood, carefully painted to resemble the original sufficiently enough to pass a cursory inspection.

During their exercise period on the afternoon of Wednesday 13 August, and screened by their comrades, Captains Dufour and Imit lifted the manhole cover and climbed into the drain taking the original bolt with them. Behind them the cover was replaced and 'secured' with the copy. When night fell the two men then pushed the cover upwards, lifting it and breaking the glass bolt in the process. Clearing the debris away as best they could they replaced the manhole cover and after screwing the original bolt back into place ran to the park wall and climbed over it to freedom, remaining at large for several days before being recaptured.

The attempt was repeated on 16 August, when Lieutenants Steinmetz and Larive again used the drain as a hiding place from which to begin their escape

Close-up of the drainage manhole cover within the park, the starting point for several Dutch escape attempts. (Author)

attempt. This time the plan was slightly more refined. One of their comrades – Lieutenant Gerrit Dames – having openly cut a hole in the wire fence, waited until he had been spotted by one of the guards and then at the top of his voice shouted 'Run!' at the undergrowth, before allowing himself to be taken by the Germans, leading them to believe that they had caught the third man in a Dutch breakout. Again waiting until darkness before they emerged from concealment, the two men clambered over the wall and, deciding to avoid Colditz railway station, walked to nearby Leisnig where they caught the early-morning train to Dresden. Changing trains in Nuremberg, their ultimate destination was Singen, from where they intended walking across the border.

Unlike their comrades, and despite a last-minute scare when they stumbled upon a German border patrol, they made it safely into neutral territory, the first of the Dutch officers to make a successful 'home run'. But even as the furore over their escape began to die down, the camp's reputation received another damaging slight when news reached Colditz that a Polish officer – Lieutenant Kroner – had escaped from the hospital at Königswartha and had successfully made his way to Warsaw, bringing the total number of escapes up to seven, a total that within a month was increased to nine when a further two Dutch officers escaped, aptly using the same method as Larive and Steinmetz. Although this number paled in comparison with the 94 thwarted escape attempts later reported by the LO3 (Hauptmann Dr Reinhold Eggers) as having taken place in the same period, they nonetheless served to give notice that Colditz's reputation as being escape-proof was a tarnished one indeed.

On the evening of 28 August Lt. Airey Neave made his first attempt to escape from Colditz by wearing an RAF uniform tailored and dyed to resemble that of a guard. Waiting until darkness, which would give his disguise a better chance of passing unwanted scrutiny by the German sentries, Neave simply marched down towards the castle gates, responding to any challenge that he had a message to deliver to Hauptmann Priem. The disguise worked well, but as he tried to select a bicycle on which to leave the castle he was surrounded by guards who had finally taken notice of his 'un-Germanic bearing'. At the following morning's roll-call, and with the would-be escaper confined to the cells, Priem took great pleasure in informing the British contingent that their comrade would not be returning to them, and that 'Gefreiter Neave' had been sent to the Russian Front.

As summer drew to a close, the camp authorities began to flirt with the idea of securing a propaganda coup by enlisting prisoners as voluntary workers. Unfortunately for the Germans however, the scheme failed drastically, possibly in part owing to the fact that the term which they used to signify this co-operation – *Mitarbeit* – was translated as 'collaboration', with negative connotations in any language.

The contempt with which the French, in particular, treated these overtures is best exemplified by an officer who one day, to the dismay of many of his fellow prisoners, loudly proclaimed that he would gladly work for a hundred Germans rather than a single Frenchman. Surprised by this announcement, and expecting that as a civilian the man had been an engineer or chemist, someone who would be valuable in Germany's manufacturing industry, the officer in charge of the parade called him forward and asked him to reiterate his name and

Photograph from the file of Lt. Airey Neave, taken during his captivity at Spangenberg (Oflag IX-A). (IWM, HU 086547)

occupation. After a pregnant pause the silence was broken by the reply 'Paul Durant, undertaker'!

The late autumn of 1941 saw the arrival of a new type of prisoner. Although the civilian, Howard Gee, had already been given some form of quasi-military status in order to justify his incarceration in Oflag IV-C, the new captive was by no stretch of the imagination a soldier, and was in fact a journalist. Ordinarily the fate of a captive reporter would not have troubled the German high command, but Giles Samuel Romilly was not merely a journalist, he was also a nephew by marriage of Winston Spencer-Churchill, the British Prime Minister, and thus it was believed that he had an inherent value as a potential hostage. A reflection of Romilly's perceived importance can be seen in the fact that the *Führerhauptquartier* (*Führer* Headquarters) in Berlin issued a detailed regimen for his treatment which was far more restrictive than that of the other prisoners. He had no exercise privileges in the castle park, his whereabouts had to be logged on an hourly basis and all guard posts were issued with copies of his file photograph in order that he would be recognized on sight.

For Kommandant Schmidt this was firmly underlined by the stark order that came from Berlin curtly informing him that should any harm befall Romilly whilst he was being held at Colditz both the Colonel and his security Chief would pay with their lives, and as other military prisoners with similar backgrounds all found themselves being later transferred to Colditz it was this odd semi-status which gave them the name by which they are most often referred to today: '*Die Prominenten*' (the celebrities).

Spartan accommodation. This cell was occupied by Captain David, the Earl Haig. Although the bed is of later, East German manufacture, the wooden furnishings are contemporary. (Author)

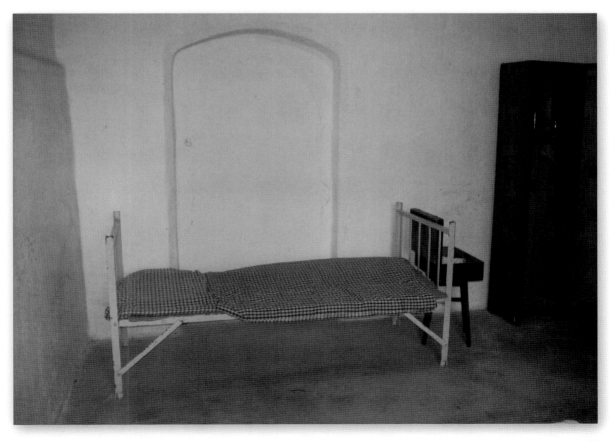

In early December the camp was rocked by the news of the Japanese attack on Pearl Harbor and the American entry into the war. For the British and Commonwealth prisoners in Colditz this could easily have meant a considerable worsening in their position as up until this point the United States had acted in the role of protecting power for British interests. Now, as a belligerent, she could no longer do so. For almost a week the situation was in a state of limbo as fierce negotiations and diplomatic overtures took place behind the scenes, which resulted in the Swiss Confederation agreeing to represent the interests of Britain, the Commonwealth and the United States in addition to those of Germany, which already fell under the Swiss remit.

After a bad start to the month, which saw a number of Dutch escape attempts being thwarted by the guards, the year closed on a positive note for the prisoners on 17 December when a group of five French officers were sent for treatment to the town dentist. On leaving the surgery, three of them suddenly bolted for freedom, running in separate directions. For their two escorts the situation was untenable. One clearly had to stay with the remaining Frenchmen, but his colleague could in no way pursue three fugitives simultaneously and so they used the dentist's telephone to warn the duty officer at the castle.

Emergency measures were immediately put in operation, with the codeword '*Mausfalle*' now being spoken into more than a dozen telephone receivers. The codeword, literally translated as 'mousetrap' was an activation signal warning local police, garrison troops, security and civil defence forces that there had been an escape and to alert them to the possibility of fugitives trying to slip through their areas of responsibility. Accordingly, levels of security – especially on trains and at railway stations – were intensified, but these measures notwithstanding the three Frenchmen successfully made it to freedom.

Christmas came and went, and New Year 1942 saw a change in the fortunes of the British contingent. Some weeks previously whilst in solitary confinement Pat Reid had noticed a window in the *Saalhaus* below the level of the theatre where, in theory at least, there was no room at all. Upon his release, he investigated further, and cutting through the floor underneath the stage found an empty room from which a short corridor led to an attic above the German guardhouse. A plan was soon formulated whereby a number of prisoners disguised as German officers would climb down from the attic and, descending the stairs, simply march out of the camp – after all, no one would expect the prisoners to have egress through the guardroom.

The camp theatre. Airey Neave and 'Tony' Luteijn were to begin their successful 'home run' from a room under the stage, discovered by Pat Reid. (Author)

In order that the prospective escapers be as convincing as possible, it was decided to pair two British officers with two of their Dutch counterparts, each with a fluent command of the German language, who would take on the role of the senior officer, whilst the Briton would act out the role of the subordinate. At first, two Dutch naval officers had been chosen to take part in the escape, but fearing reprisals to their families in the Netherlands they withdrew and their places were taken by Lieutenants Abraham 'Tony' Luteijn and H. G. Donkers of the Koninklijk Nederlands-Indisch Leger. The British officers – Lieutenants Airey Neave and John Hyde-Thompson – were chosen by the simple expedient that they had produced the most realistic German uniforms. After the evening roll-call on 5 January, Neave and Luteijn climbed down into the room beneath the stage and made their way to the attic above the guardhouse. Anxiously watched from the windows above, they boldly made their way past all of the sentry posts and down into the park where, changing into civilian clothes, they climbed over the wall and disappeared into the night.

The following evening it was the turn of Donkers and Hyde-Thompson, who also made it safely out of the castle but returned under escort a few days later having been arrested by a railway policeman who had earlier allowed Neave and Luteijn to pass unhindered.

Shortly after this came the news that had been anxiously awaited. Travelling towards Singen, Neave and Luteijn had successfully reached and crossed the Swiss border. Not only was this a vindication of the system of cooperation engendered by the introduction of the role of the 'escape officers', but more importantly from a morale perspective Airey Neave became the first British officer to make a 'home run'.

On 9 January 1942, the first group of French officers – some 31 men – were transferred from Colditz to Oflag IV-D at Elsterhorst, and, given that a number of them had been particularly involved in the construction of the French tunnel, one that the Germans had been fruitlessly seeking for several months, their thoughts turned immediately to infiltrators and collaborators.

Entrance to the shaft in the clock tower used by the French to gain access to the wine cellar. (Author)

Close-up of the entrance of the section of the French tunnel that began in the German wine cellar. This arduous work was achieved mainly using home-made tools, and at any one time up to 22 men were employed in disposing of the spoil. (Author)

Since their initial construction had been discovered and blocked off by the Germans, the French contingent had reopened their original excavation and, guided by a map supplied by the British, had been slowly and steadily tunnelling their way to what they thought was a sealed vault under the chapel. From the wine cellar they dug their way upwards into a crawlspace beneath the chapel floor, and using home-made saws were then forced to cut their way through a number of wooden supports before making their way across the chapel, at which stage they finally realized that there was in fact no vault. The Frenchmen were faced with a stark decision: either to abandon the work of several months or to press on regardless and extend the tunnel into the eastern slopes above the castle park, from where the entire French contingent could attempt to escape in a single mass breakout. They decided to press on.

Over a period of weeks the French began a refurbishment of the existing tunnel, and, instead of the fat-based lamps that they had hitherto been using, they attached a spur to the castle's power supply and installed not only full electric lighting in the tunnel, but also a warning system in the chapel. This last stage of excavation was interminably slow, not only because the tunnel was being extended through loose rock and soil, but also the fact that the spoil had to be brought back the length of the tunnel and up to the top of the clock tower. At one stage some 22 men were involved solely in this task. The Frenchmen were now only a short distance from freedom, but even as they began their final preparations a party of guards under Stabsfeldwebel Gephard discovered the concealed entrance at the top of the clock tower, and potentially the most audacious attempt to escape from Colditz came to an end.

Buoyed by Neave and Luteijn's successful escape and undeterred by the discovery of the French tunnel, the spring of 1942 saw many prisoners attempting to escape from Colditz. Whilst some were caught in the act, and others were recaptured having spent some time on the run, the law of averages inevitably betokened success and on 26 April five officers escaped from the

military hospital at Gnaschwitz. Four of them were ultimately recaptured but the fifth, Captain Louis Rémy of the Belgian army, successfully evaded all attempts at recapture and eventually made his way to Algeciras in Spain.

On 19 May a further reorganization within Colditz occurred, with all bar 40 of the Polish contingent being transferred to another camp, followed a week later by 125 French and Belgians who were sent to Oflag X-C at Lübeck. Early in June, Brian Paddon received a summons to court-martial proceedings for an incident at one of the camps where he had been previously held. Despite the heavy security, he managed to slip away from his guards and made his way to Danzig where he stowed away on board a Swedish freighter. Once the vessel had left German territorial waters, Paddon turned himself over to the ship's captain who decided that he should turn the ship around and return the fugitive to his captors. For an awful moment it seemed as if the Englishman's escape would be thwarted at the moment of his success, but wiser heads prevailed and the ship continued to Sweden. His flight had certainly lived up to his camp nickname of 'Never a dull moment'.

Kommandant Gläsche

At around this time Schmidt was replaced by Edgar Gläsche, an officer of a totally different stamp. Whilst Schmidt was content to let the camp run itself, intervening only when necessary, his successor was more of a 'hands-on' type, insisting that the prisoners' truculence be met with punitive action on the part of the camp authorities, introducing *Strafappelle* (punishment roll-calls) that were often conducted in the early hours of the morning, thus disrupting the prisoners' routine.

Oberst Edgar Gläsche, Schmidt's successor as *Kommandant*. (IWM, HU 086540)

Autumn 1942 saw an escalation of the constant struggle between captors and captives, when on 9 September, in the first of a number of escape attempts, three British and three Dutch officers managed to escape via the storeroom disguised as a group of Polish workers and their German escort. Once safely away from the castle, and following the procedure that had worked so well for Neave and Luteijn, the fugitives paired off and made their escape from the town. Four of the men were soon recaptured but the remaining pair – Flight Lieutenant Hedley 'Bill' Fowler (Royal Australian Air Force) and Lieutenant Damiaem van Doorninck (Royal Dutch Navy) managed to evade capture, eventually making their way across the Swiss border at Tuttlingen.

On the evening of 7 October one of a number of tragedies in the story of Colditz began to play itself out when a group of seven prisoners arrived at Colditz without the prior knowledge of either the *Kommandant* or any of his staff. On requesting further instructions from Oberkommando der Wehrmacht (OKW), Gläsche was told to keep them incommunicado, locked up where they would have no contact with the rest of the

---

E **LE MÉTRO**

Originally intended as an attempt to find a non-existent crypt under the chapel, the French tunnel, or 'Le Métro' as it became known, stretched from the German wine cellars, under the chapel and out towards the wire fences overlooking the park, but was discovered as it was nearing completion. In its latter stages the tunnel boasted its own electric lighting system, alarm and mini railway to facilitate the removal of spoil.

prisoners. The men were British commandos, the survivors of Operation *Musketoon* – an attack on the hydroelectric plant at Glomfjord in Norway. The next morning, whilst waiting to be photographed by Johannes Lange they managed to establish contact with two of the British prisoners, explaining who they were and what their mission had been before they had been captured. This was information that Capt. Rupert Barry was eventually able to relay to British Military Intelligence in London by sending a coded message to his wife in England.

The commandos, under the command of Canadian officer Captain Graeme Black, remained in Colditz for less than a week before being sent to Berlin for interrogation by the Gestapo, a process that can have resulted only in the men being tortured. On 18 October, Hitler issued his infamous '*Kommandobefehl*' or 'Commando Order', which ordered the summary execution of all Allied commandos, irrespective of the circumstances of their capture. Although the British officers in Colditz were able to warn the Swiss authorities about the fate that awaited Black and his men there was no time for them to intervene. On 22 October they were transferred to KZ Sachsenhausen near Berlin and subsequently executed. In a possible attempt to muddy the waters, instructions were sent back to Colditz to the effect that should any letters addressed to any of the dead men be received at the castle, they should immediately be returned to sender, marked '*Geflohen*' (escaped).

Whilst the fateful drama of Operation *Musketoon* played out its final act, within Colditz plans proceeded apace for another, this time exclusively British, escape attempt. After the evening roll-call on October 14, British officers Major Ronnie Littledale, Capt. Pat Reid, Lieutenant-Commander 'Billie' Stephens and Canadian Flying Officer 'Hank' Wardle cautiously made their way to the prisoners' kitchens. The plan was to use a window that overlooked the *Kommandantur* as a means to get into the German courtyard and then break into one of the storage buildings, from which they would then abseil down the outer wall of the castle and make a dash for freedom. As the kitchen window afforded a limited view of the courtyard, the plan was refined by the participation of a musical ensemble conducted by Wing Commander Douglas Bader that was playing in the *Saalhaus* overlooking the entire *Kommandantur*. The trick was simple – Bader would watch out for the guard patrols and would signal the all-clear by having the musicians stop playing when the coast was clear for the escapers to make their move.

Reid and Wardle were the first pair out of the kitchens, making their way to a small cellar near the German offices where the men could hide whilst Reid attempted to break into the target building. Finding the door to be firmly locked, they needed to find an alternative way out and in the cellar found a small chute that opened out above the dry moat below the castle's southern wall. All attempts to negotiate the flue met with failure as each of the men was wearing several layers of clothing. With the clock ticking against them they stripped naked and passed their clothes up through the flue, making it out into the dry moat after much struggling. Partially dressing, they quickly made their way down to the park where they finished reassembling their disguises as foreign labourers and climbed over the wall. The following day a passer-by spotted a pile of camp-issue blankets under some bushes and the alarm was raised, but the four were well on their way to freedom. Reid and Wardle crossed the Swiss border on the night of Sunday 18 October whilst Littledale and Stephens crossed over the following evening.

The flue through which Reid, Wardle, Littledale and Stephens had to climb naked in order to make their escape into the dry moat from the *Kommandantur* and then into the park, where they split up and each group made its bid for freedom. (Author)

During the weeks that followed, the bars of Colditz were continually rattled as a dozen officers each – albeit unsuccessfully – tried their hand at escape. But German claims that Oflag IV-C was escape-proof were once again dented in late November when two submariners – Chief Petty Officers Wally Hammond and Don Lister – petitioned Oberst Gläsche to the effect that they were not officers in the strictest sense of the word and thus they were being held at Colditz illegally and should be immediately transferred to an alternate camp. From a legal standpoint, Hammond and Lister were completely in the right and the *Kommandant* had no other alternative but to endorse the transfer request, with the two men being sent to the massive complex at Lamsdorf (now Lambinowice in Poland) that held over 400,000 Allied prisoners. Having learnt their lessons at Colditz well, both men then simply absconded from a work party and after several adventures they crossed the Swiss border on 19 December.

For the inmates of Colditz, the year almost ended on a high note when the French short-circuited the lights in their quarters, which resulted in a local electrician called Willi Pöhnert being called in to make the repairs. After a short while the electrician left the building and headed for the main gate, mumbling to the guard that he had forgotten some tools that he needed to complete the repairs. At the next post, the sentry asked to see the man's pass, and when he couldn't produce one the final escape attempt of the year collapsed. Pöhnert was in fact a Frenchman – Lieutenant Pérodeau – who, being of similar height and build, had disguised himself as the hapless electrician. The power cut had been an elaborately staged ruse to bring Pöhnert into the castle and allow the doppelgänger to make his escape.

Kommandant Prawitt

The year of 1942 was the high water mark for the inmates of Colditz. Over the course of 80 or so escape attempts, 16 men – seven British, five French, three Dutch and one Belgian – had all made 'home runs' with a further three successfully escaping whilst in transit. It was an impressive record, one that would never be bettered, and as news of Allied successes in Russia and North Africa filtered their way into the camp a new sense of optimism began to pervade the prisoners' quarters, especially when columns of smoke could be seen on the north-western horizon coming from the IG Farben chemical plant at Leuna, which had been attacked by the Allies as part of their strategic bombing campaign.

Within the camp, relations between the Allied officers and their captors soon began to break down, with Gläsche resurrecting a dispute over the entitlement of German officers to receive the salute from the prisoners, and then trying to stamp his authority on the camp by reorganizing the system of roll-calls, introducing bells that would signal when a roll-call was imminent. He then went one stage further – perhaps too far – firstly by installing a photographer in a position from where he could take pictures of the entire courtyard and thus capture the image of any troublemakers for use at their court martial, and secondly by setting up a machine-gun position which could likewise cover the entire area and, if necessary, be used against the prisoners. When the prisoners discovered the new measures discipline began to slide unerringly towards insubordination, and on 15 February 1943 Kommandant Gläsche was relieved of his command and transferred to the Ukraine.

Unlike his two predecessors, the new *Kommandant* of Colditz, Oberstleutnant Gerhard Prawitt, was a combat soldier who had been invalided out of frontline service after suffering a stomach wound during the French campaign, after which he had served with the *Führerreserve* in Warsaw until December 1942 when he was sent to Colditz preparatory to his taking over from Oberst Gläsche as *Kommandant*. At 43, Prawitt was closer in age to his charges than either of his predecessors, and he was also more attuned to the prisoners' attitude towards their duty to escape. He was determined from the outset to take a firmer line than either Schmidt or Gläsche had, immediately embarking on a modernization of the castle's defences. As one hapless guard wrote: 'On the days when we weren't on watch, we all had to put on gloves and fit more barbed wire.' With a veteran's eye, and determined that there would be no further escapes on his watch, Prawitt then studied previous escape attempts with the intent of blocking all possible exits and finally making Colditz 'escape-proof'. Firstly, the existing barbed wire was reinforced and refurbished with more being placed across the east-facing slopes that led down from the castle into the park, and then in order to prevent the prisoners from using the road entrance into the German courtyard as an avenue of escape a sentry post with a gated catwalk was established to block any egress. To supplement the sentry posts on the other side of the castle, an additional watchtower cum machine-gun position was built on the lower terrace at the junction of the northern and western walls. Finally, and aware of the length of time that it had taken for both Schmidt and Gläsche to detect and uncover several of the escape tunnels dug by the prisoners, Prawitt ordered the installation of a number of microphones and listening devices to give the guards an advantage over the would-be escapers.

Outwardly, Prawitt's flurry of activity was viewed as the actions of a martinet, but unlike many in his position the new *Kommandant* realized that as a result of the spate of military disasters at the front, replacements would urgently need to be found and that it was only a matter of time before the able-bodied members of his garrison company would be culled off and sent to the front line. They would be replaced by the old, the young and the infirm, who would have to pit themselves against perhaps the most hardened escapers currently in German captivity.

In this regard Oberstleutnant Prawitt was soon proved to be prescient, as shortly after assuming command of Colditz he was advised that, subject to a medical examination, many of his garrison would be reassigned to combat units and that their places in a reduced garrison would be assumed by third-line elements, the majority of whom had not passed through anything more than the most rudimentary of basic training, and who were to be armed with a collection of captured and outdated weapons for which there was only a limited supply of ammunition. Had the prisoners but known this, and attempted a mass breakout, it is highly doubtful if the guards would have been able to stop them.

On 15 February 1943 Giles Romilly was joined by another prisoner who the Germans believed shared a similar background – Lieutenant Michael Alexander. In August the previous year, whilst on detached service, Alexander had been captured in North Africa following a raid behind enemy lines. Dressed in a German uniform, he was almost certain to face the firing squad and in desperation exaggerated a distant family relationship to Field Marshal Harold Alexander, the newly appointed Commander-in-Chief Middle East Command. After a spell in Italian custody, and with his captors believing that he was in fact the Field Marshal's nephew, Alexander soon found himself whisked to Berlin and eventually to Colditz, where he became Romilly's cellmate.

Within the camp, the new regime met with limited success, in that the prisoners were in no way intimidated by Prawitt's more aggressive stance than either of his predecessors and within the first six months of the year a total of 14 escape attempts had been made. Almost all of these ended in failure owing to a combination of factors. Firstly, it must be said that Prawitt's updating of the castle's defences were proving to be a difficult rampart for the prisoners to breach, but also with increasing numbers of Allied air raids taking place over German soil, the scale of the '*Mausfalle*', in which fugitives would be pursued by a mixture of party and civil defence formations, had by now been replaced with a larger and more refined operation named '*Hasenjagd*' or 'Hare Drive'. Coupled with the people's natural distrust of strangers, this inevitably made travelling through the German countryside that much more dangerous.

Lieutenant 'Mike' Sinclair. Perhaps the most persistent escaper to have been held at Colditz, he was respectfully known to his captors as '*der rote Fuchs*' – the red fox. (IWM, HU 049550)

Despite his tightening of castle security, there was nothing that Prawitt could do to prevent prisoners from being officially sent to facilities outside of the castle, whether to various hospitals for medical assistance that was unavailable in Colditz or to Dresden for legal proceedings. During the first half of the year, a further four men were able to make a successful 'home run'. Amongst them was an Indian, Dr Biren Mazumdar, who went on hunger strike until his petition to be transferred to an 'Indians only' camp in France was granted, from where he escaped and joined the Resistance. There was also an Irishman, Dr Ion Ferguson, who was transferred to Stalag IV-D at Torgau where he gradually faked symptoms of insanity and was repatriated in January 1945.

The Franz Josef escape
In April 1943, two British Officers – Lieutenants Albert 'Mike' Sinclair and 'Monty' Bissell – approached Dick Howe, the

A decorated veteran of World War I, Stabsfeldwebel Fritz Rothenberger was held in awe by many of the troops under his command and it was this reverence that Sinclair intended to capitalize upon in what has become known as 'the Franz Josef escape'. (IWM, HU 049544)

British escape officer, with a novel suggestion for what had the potential to develop into a mass breakout. Up until that point, they reminded Howe, disguises had been used in an attempt to pass off a potential escaper as a member of the castle garrison so that they could leave the camp and hopefully make their way to freedom. Their argument, however, was to take this premise and turn it on its head. The aim of the plan was for Sinclair to impersonate Stabsfeldwebel Rothenberger, the senior NCO in charge of the nightly inspections on the eastern sentry posts, and then for 'Rothenberger' to replace a number of sentries with suitably disguised prisoners. If successful, this would give them a period of about five minutes during which as many prisoners as possible would try to escape through the now-opened gates. When the men were on the run, Sinclair and his guards would 'set off in pursuit' sowing further confusion by ordering any real guards back to the castle to gather reinforcements.

The sheer audacity of the plan appealed to Howe and received his unqualified approval, thus over the next few months the 25-year-old Sinclair threw himself into learning all he could about the elderly NCO – his accent, his gait, his mannerisms – everything that would aid him in his performance and convince the guards that they were dealing with their superior. Whilst Sinclair's preparations were made with the single-mindedness that had already made him a legend amongst his peers, other preparations were also being made, not only in the manufacture of accurate uniforms and the requisite paperwork for the three ersatz guards, but also a replica of Rothenberger's trademark bushy moustache from which derived his camp nickname – 'Franz Josef' – after the former Austrian emperor. The plan also called for a first wave of 20 escapers, all of whom would require suitable civilian clothing in addition to both identity and travel papers as well as local maps. It was a mammoth task that kept Colditz's forgers and tailors busy for several months.

Should the plan be successful, Bissell and his colleagues would then lower themselves onto the terrace and use the now-open gateway to escape down to the park and over the wall. Dependent on how quickly the Germans reacted, further prisoners – in groups of ten, and albeit not so well prepared in terms of clothing and papers – would attempt to follow suit. Given their estimated window of opportunity, Sinclair and Bissell hoped that between twenty and fifty men would be able to break out in the confusion.

As summer wore on and preparations continued, news was received of the escape and subsequent fate of the 65 British officers from Oflag VII-B at Eichstätt, but as Flt. Lt. Jack Best was later to recall: 'The point of escaping is not necessarily to get back to one's unit and rejoin the war… The point

F THE FRANZ JOSEF ESCAPE

On 4 September 1943, the British prisoners attempted perhaps the most audacious of all the attempts to escape from Colditz. Lieutenant Mike Sinclair, dressed as Stabsfeldwebel Rothenberger, a senior German NCO, attempted to replace a number of sentries with disguised prisoners and open a route along the eastern flank of the castle through which up to 50 British POWs would make a bid for freedom. With the alarm having been raised, and additional guards rushing through the gate, here we see the two Rothenbergers confronting each other. In the scuffle that ensued, Sinclair was shot in the chest, his wounding effectively signalling the end of the escape attempt.

is to get out and give them a problem. The more people the bigger the problem – it ties them up, it keeps them busy.'

On the evening of 4 September all was ready. After the evening roll-call, Sinclair, accompanied by John Hyde-Thompson and Lance Pope, two fluent German speakers who were playing the role of the replacement guards, entered the sickbay and climbed out of a specially prepared window onto the terrace. The performance of Sinclair's life was about to begin.

Making their way through the shadows, the group rounded the north-eastern corner of the terrace and approached the first guard post. Above them, lookouts let out a collective sigh of relief as, casting a critical eye over the sentry, Sinclair told him that he was relieved of duty and ordered him back to the guardroom; the first obstacle had been surmounted, and only the gate itself remained to be negotiated. The remaining guards looked askance at each other as the senior NCO approached, wondering why Rothenberger was conducting his inspection earlier than usual.

Marching up to the sentry box, Sinclair told the guard that there had been an escape attempt on the other side of the castle and ordered him to return to the guardhouse for further instructions. Believing that he was dealing with the real Rothenberger the man saluted and marched away, his place being taken by Pope. Sinclair then ascended the catwalk above the gate and repeated his orders to the guard there who climbed down, his place being taken by Hyde-Thompson. In the British quarters it looked as if the audacious plan was actually going to work, and a single German soldier now stood in the way of success.

Upon receiving his new orders, the third sentry answered that he was under strict orders not to leave his post under any circumstances, but 'Rothenberger' was having none of it. Raising his voice, he began shouting at the hapless German, who stood his ground and asked to see the *Stabsfeldwebel*'s pass. Despite the months of meticulous planning, it transpired that the colour of the passes had been changed that very evening, and aware that something

With the decision to effectively turn Colditz into an 'Anglo-American' camp, prisoners of other nationalities were sent to other camps throughout the German Reich. Here, a column of Frenchmen bid *'adieu'* to their former prison. (Courtesy Australian War Memorial, Canberra – P01608-002)

was amiss the guard hit the alarm bell. There are several conflicting accounts of exactly what happened in the ensuing confusion, but within seconds two further groups of Germans, including the real Rothenberger, began to converge on the gateway.

His anger rising, Sinclair was not about to concede defeat and continued to abuse the hapless guard, hoping to bully him into obedience. But as the additional guards began to arrive, a scuffle ensued that was stopped only by the report of a pistol shot as Sinclair slumped to the ground with a bullet in his chest. Sinclair eventually recovered from his wound, whilst the guard who shot him was quietly transferred to the Eastern Front.

Conditions worsen

The failure of the 'Franz Josef' escape, and the fact that an escapee was severely injured, marked a period of change both within Colditz and within Germany itself. Firstly, in May 1943, OKW had decided that Oflag IV-C would become a camp for Anglo-American prisoners only, and over the course of the summer all other nationalities were moved to other camps throughout the Third Reich. Secondly, the intensification of the Allied bombing offensive and the subsequent labelling of Allied airmen as 'terrorists' had meant that strangers in German territory were more likely to be assaulted and arrested rather than allowed to pass on by with a friendly wave. In effect, it was becoming safer for the prisoners to remain within the castle walls rather than to make a bid for freedom, risking mistreatment and possibly death at the hands of lynch mobs hunting downed aircrew. On 7 June, the Dutch contingent had left Colditz for the camp at Stanislau in the Ukraine, whilst from 6–12 July the Franco-Belgian officers were moved to Oflag X-C at Lübeck, with the remainder of the Poles being sent in August to Oflag IV-B at Dössel-Warburg. At their respective new camps, all three nationalities made life difficult for their captors, and, whilst a significant number of Dutch and French prisoners were able to make individual 'home runs', fortune refused to smile on the Poles. On their arrival, they began extending a tunnel originally dug by Canadian POWs, who had themselves been transferred to Colditz. On the evening of 19 September, 47 men broke out of the camp, of whom nine successfully made their way to freedom – the remaining 38, including five former inmates of Colditz, were quickly recaptured, handed over to the Gestapo and murdered at KZ Buchenwald.

The new year, 1944, saw a marked change in the prisoners' conditions as a number of snap searches were carried out, not by members of the garrison company, a number of whom were suspected of being more than amenable to bribery, but by members of the SS brought in specifically for the purpose. On 28 January, Canadian officer Lieutenant 'Bill' Millar used the cover of an air raid alarm to make his way into the German courtyard and conceal himself under an army truck, which eventually drove out of the castle with the Canadian hanging on underneath. It was the last time that he was seen alive, and it was only after the end of the war that his possible fate was determined.

On 2 March Heinrich Himmler authorized a document simply known as 'Aktion K' – the 'K' standing for *Kügel* or 'bullet'. Its terms were simple – any escapees who were recaptured and who were not required for 'essential' war work would be taken to KZ Mauthausen. Upon arrival, those prisoners whose names were marked with a 'K' would be immediately separated from the others, and instead of being registered in the camp records would be taken directly to a room near the crematoria and executed, their bodies being immediately burned. The sole exceptions to 'Aktion K' were Anglo-American prisoners who had the dubious honour of having their cases 'viewed on individual merit', although it is doubtful that any exceptions were ever made. In Millar's case, it is believed that he was recaptured near Lamsdorf sometime during the summer of 1944 and after being handed over to the Sicherheitsdienst (SD) he was murdered at Mauthausen shortly afterwards.

Despite the clear threat of what could happen in the event of their recapture, it is clear that the inmates of Colditz took Flt. Lt. Jack Best's maxim to heart and remained persistent in their attempts to escape the castle. With the exception of a number of officers who were repatriated on medical grounds having faked their symptoms, there would be no more 'home runs'. It may be that these attempts could now be considered to have served a dual purpose. Firstly, a successful escape would cause an obvious problem for the camp authorities but also, and just as importantly, the planning of the escape

The grave of Lieutenant 'Mike' Sinclair. After the war, Sinclair's remains were exhumed from the graveyard in Colditz, and reinterred at the Commonwealth War Graves Commission Cemetery in the Berlin suburb of Charlottenburg. For his conduct during his captivity, he was posthumously awarded the DSO. (Author)

and its execution served to maintain the morale of the POWs, giving them a tangible objective upon which they could focus their attention.

For Sinclair, however, to plan an escape was to follow it through and almost a year to the day after his wounding during the 'Franz Josef' escape he was caught trying to clamber over the wire fence in the park. It was his eighth and penultimate escape attempt. A scant three weeks later, he was again in the park during the exercise period, and turning to Lieutenant 'Gris' Davies-Scourfield, his closest friend, he said 'Goodbye Grismond, it's now or never'. With that he ran for the fence and began to climb. Sinclair made it to the top of the wire before the guards noticed him and as he jumped to the ground the first shot rang out. Dodging and weaving he ignored the guards' cries ordering him to halt, and he began to run uphill towards the stone wall. More shots rang out, but visibly tiring, Sinclair continued to run and then staggered and fell. As the guards came up to him they turned over his body and saw that Sinclair had made a 'home run' in the most tragic of circumstances – one of the bullets had struck him on the elbow and ricocheted into his heart, killing him instantly. As a sign of the regard with which Kommandant Prawitt held his persistent and erstwhile adversary, Sinclair was buried with full military honours in Colditz cemetery, his coffin borne by the eight members of his regiment held at Colditz and draped with a Union Jack made by members of the garrison. He was later reinterred at the British Military Cemetery in the Berlin suburb of Charlottenburg, and for his courage and resolution during his captivity was posthumously awarded the Distinguished Service Order (DSO).

The latter part of 1944 saw the arrival in Colditz of a number of individual prisoners. They included those declared as being '*Deutschfeindlich*' such as Lieutenant-Colonel David Stirling DSO, co-founder of the SAS, Colonel Florimund Duke (who at 49-years-old was the oldest serving American paratrooper) and Captain Charles Upham, NZEF, recipient of the Victoria Cross and Bar for his actions in Crete and North Africa. There were also an increasing number of *Prominenten* such as Lieutenant George, the Viscount Lascelles, Captain John, the Master of Elphinstone and Lieutenant Max de Hamel, nephews respectively of King George VI, Queen Elizabeth and Winston Churchill. Another new arrival was Captain David, the Earl Haig, son of the World War I field marshal.

The end draws near

With the Allies now making considerable progress on all fronts and the 'high-security' status of Oflag IV-C being more symbolic than real, the German government still continued to use Colditz as a repository for important prisoners. In January 1945, six French generals were transferred from Königstein (Oflag IV-B), although one of their number, General Mesny, was shot in Dresden 'whilst trying to escape', and the following month General Tadeusz Komorowski, commander of the Polish Home Army, and a number of his senior aides arrived in the castle, having been held captive by the Germans since the collapse of the Warsaw Uprising the previous autumn.

Despite the fact that the war was now entering its final throes, Mike Sinclair's legacy remained a tangible one. Flight Lieutenant Jack Best, Flight Lieutenant 'Bill' Goldfinch and Lieutenant Anthony Rolt worked on perhaps the greatest 'what if' in the story of Colditz. Beginning in May 1944, using planks of wood culled from beds and floorboards and with a covering made from bedsheets, in a concealed workshop in one of the upper attics they had been building a two-man glider. When launched by the dropping of a bathtub filled with concrete, it was hoped that it would carry its passengers out over the castle and across the Mulde to the meadows on the western bank of the river, giving them a significant head start over any German pursuit. Although the plan was overtaken by events and never flew – the original glider disappearing sometime in the after-war years – a modern British television documentary built a replica of the glider and proved that it would have indeed flown and carried its passengers away from the castle.

Having received few of the food parcels to which they were entitled, the prisoners' position worsened on 26 February, when 1,500 French prisoners arrived at Colditz from Königstein, immediately prompting a drastic cut in rations. This indirectly affected the German guards, who were themselves becoming increasingly dependent upon what little food that they could obtain by barter with the prisoners. With the Third Reich in a state of terminal collapse, and with the Allied air forces bombing around the clock, the medieval walls offered a refuge from the maelstrom outside. Its occupants waited to see which of the Allied powers would be the first to reach the town.

Although they couldn't know it, preparations were indeed under way to relieve the castle; Lebrun, now serving on the staff of the French 1ère Armée, initially received permission to organize an armoured column to punch through the collapsing German lines and race the 600km to Colditz, but the plan was scrapped in the wake of political decisions reached at the Yalta Conference that began on 4 February. Separately, the Anglo-Americans began organizing three-man teams to be dropped near selected camps and establishing contact with the senior officers, after which they would arrange weapons drops and organize them against their captors. Three such teams were allocated to Colditz, but before the plan could be put into operation, the castle was liberated by elements of the US 1st Army.

On 6 April, probably the last of the *Prominenten* arrived in Colditz. Lieutenant John G. Winant, USAAF, was the son of the United States' ambassador to Great Britain, and had been captured after his B-17 'Flying Fortress' had been shot down over Munich. Winant's arrival seemed to herald the final moments of Oflag IV-C as rumours began to abound of American spearheads pushing forward in the wake of the columns of German troops already fleeing through the town. But these were but rumours and an SS battalion soon arrived in Colditz, its commander having orders to liaise with Kommandant Prawitt in the defence of the area, and agreeing with Prawitt's suggestion that the castle garrison remain solely responsible for the defence of the castle whilst the SS deployed in the town itself – an agreement that undoubtedly saved many lives.

Germany was in a state of collapse, and on 12 April Prawitt received an unsigned letter from the Office of the Reichsführer-SS instructing him to make the *Prominenten* ready for transportation to a secret location in the early hours of the following morning, it was obvious that all pretence had been dropped and they were now simply hostages. In a heated exchange with the senior Allied officers, Prawitt protested that they were being moved for their safety and that he and his officers were being held responsible for their lives in the event of any of the men escaping, but when he admitted that the guard detail would be drawn from SS personnel, chaos erupted. Whilst the men assembled in the German courtyard, Colonel Willie Tod, the senior British officer, turned to the shaken *Kommandant* and assured him that should anything happen to the prisoners, he would ensure that Prawitt would be arraigned before an Allied tribunal. Tod then told John Elphinstone that the Swiss authorities had been warned, and that they would be following the *Prominenten*. He then demanded and received an assurance from Prawitt that the security officer, Dr Eggers, would accompany the convoy and obtain a written statement from each officer confirming their safe arrival. As the buses drove out of the castle, Giles Romilly stood and turning to his companions drawled: 'I just thought that you'd all like to know that today is Friday the 13th.'

Driving through the bombed-out ruins of Dresden, the small convoy drove to Königstein and then continued to Laufen in Bavaria, which had by this stage of the war been redesignated as an internment camp. Here the Swiss authorities made the camp commandant aware that the British government held him responsible for the men's safety. This threat became academic on 2 May when they were once again moved, this time to Markt Pongau near Salzburg. Here, the men were met by Obergruppenführer Gottlob Berger, the SS officer responsible for all POWs within the Third Reich. Berger soon relayed the amazing news that he had defied Hitler's order to have the *Prominenten* shot. Understandably nervous about the reaction from Berlin, Berger allowed himself to be persuaded by the Swiss that the best way to ensure his future would be to release them into Swiss custody. The following day, led by a Buick draped with the Swiss flag and with a heavy escort of SS grenadiers they set out for the American lines. Moving cautiously through the final stages of the German *Götterdämmerung*, and fearing that an SS execution squad was on their tail, they eventually reached the headquarters of the US 53rd Division at Innsbruck. They were free at last.

With the departure of the *Prominenten* things at Colditz began to slowly unravel, beginning with the receipt of the 'Z-R Befehl' on the morning of 14 April. This order, more fully written as 'Zerstörung-Raümig Befehl', was for the recipient to destroy the camp facilities and for the prisoners to be evacuated to the east. Knowing that relief was at hand, the senior Allied officers refused to move their charges and after a heated debate with Prawitt they persuaded him to hand over control of the castle to the prisoners, although to deceive the SS troops in the town, normal routine was to be outwardly maintained. Prawitt then ordered the garrison to defend the castle against any attackers, with the codicil that they not open fire against the prisoners or American troops.

Early on 15 April, a Task Force of the 9th US Armoured Division under the command of Colonel Leo Shaughnessy arrived on the outskirts of Colditz. Although Shaughnessy's primary objective was to provide flank cover for the drive on Leipzig, he had also been advised of the presence of a number of POWs in the area and was ordered to secure their release if both practicable and possible. Advancing under a covering artillery barrage, Shaughnessy ordered his gunners to concentrate on the most prominent feature on the far bank of the Mulde, 'one of the towers of a large and imposing castle', and as a few ranging shots impacted on the castle buildings a number of French and British flags appeared from the upper windows, revealing the position of the POWs. Quickly, Shaughnessy called his battery commander and ordered him to immediately cease fire, his quick reactions preventing the bombardment of the castle with a mixture of incendiary and high-explosive shells.

During the night, the remainder of the SS garrison decamped from Colditz, fighting a desultory rearguard action against the advance elements of Shaughnessy's force, which gained a foothold across the Mulde shortly after dawn on the next day. As his main body of troops proceeded slowly through

the town, greeted by increasing numbers of white flags, a reconnaissance section of four men was sent up to the castle to ascertain the prisoners' situation. Within the castle, the section commander, PFC Alan H. Murphey, was greeted by a number of British prisoners placed at the main gate by Colonel Tod. Then, in the outer courtyard, he took the formal surrender of Oflag IV-C from Hauptmann Eggers, whom he then sent to his company commander under escort. Moving onward, Murphey approached the inner courtyard, ordered the German sentry to open the 'Whispering Gate', and walked into the compound unnoticed by the men wandering aimlessly around the yard. His anonymity did not last for long as it dawned upon the men that the presence of this heavily armed soldier meant that Colditz had finally been liberated and that they were free.

AFTERMATH

For some days after their liberation, the inmates of Colditz remained within the castle precincts as their various needs were attended to, and were then driven in convoy to a former Luftwaffe base near Erfurt, from where they were repatriated to Great Britain, their war over at last.

In May 1945, in accordance with the agreements reached at Yalta, Colditz was handed over to the Russians as it fell within the newly organized Soviet zone of occupation. Initially, the castle was used as a camp for displaced persons, and then in 1949 the Russians withdrew and Colditz came into the possession of the fledgling DDR, which converted the castle into a combined hospital and nursing home. During the renovations for this, much of the interior fittings were stripped out and rebuilt so that the castle only superficially resembled its former incarnation.

The summer of 1989 saw the beginning of the collapse of the DDR as first Hungary removed all border controls and then on 9 November sections of the Berlin Wall were opened, permitting free movement through both halves of the city. On 3 October 1990 the five states that comprised East Germany were integrated into the Federal Republic.

In 1996, the Gesellschaft Schloss Colditz e.V., was formed to promote the castle's cultural heritage, and the following year work began on a continuing programme of renovation. This has brought to light many artistic treasures that had lain hidden for centuries. Whilst the society organizes many cultural events and concerts throughout the year, the prisoners' area has now been developed as an 'Escape Museum' where visitors can experience at first hand the history of this forbidding edifice. Parallel to this, the *Kommandantur* was redeveloped as a 34-room youth hostel with 161 beds, which opened to the public in 2007. In 2010 the Sächsische Landesmusikakademie (Saxon Academy of Music) was transferred to Colditz.

The town of Colditz lies within easy reach by road or rail (around 40–60 minutes) of the major cities of Dresden and Leipzig, which are themselves served by the main airport at Leipzig/Halle (major airlines) and Leipzig/Altenburg (Ryanair), although it should be noted that there is no direct rail link to the town and visitors are advised to check the train timetables carefully. The German railway's website (www.bahn.de) gives an excellent planning service that advises on all connections and travel times for each stage of the journey.

For prospective visitors to the castle, the Colditz Society's full contact details can be found on their website www.schloss-colditz.com, whilst details of the youth hostel can be found at www.jugendherberge-sachsen.de.

FURTHER READING

Booker, Michael, *Collecting Colditz and its Secrets* (Grub Street, 2005)

Chancellor, Henry, *Colditz, The Definitive History* (Coronet, 2001)

Deutsche Städteatlas, *Colditz, GSV Städteatlas Verlag* (Altenbeken, 1984)

Eggers, Dr Reinhold, *Colditz, the German Story* (Robert Hale, 1961)

Neave, Airey, *They Have Their Exits* (Hodder & Stoughton, 1953)

Reid, Patrick R., *The Colditz Story* (Hodder & Stoughton, 1952)

——, *The Latter Days at Colditz* (Cassell, 2003)

——, *Colditz, the Full Story* (Macmillan, 1984)

Romilly, Giles and Alexander, Michael, *Hostages at Colditz* (Sphere, 1973)

Schädlich, Thomas, *Colditzer Schlossgeschichten* (privately published, 1992)

Stadt Colditz, *700 Jahre Stadt Colditz* (Döbeln, 1965)

Thiede, Regina and Lippmann, Renate, *Schloss Colditz* (Edition Leipzig, 2007)

INDEX